# Inside an Academic Scandal

The MIT Press's publishing mission benefits from the generosity of our donors, including Phillip and Ann Sharp.

# Inside an Academic Scandal

A Story of Fraud and Betrayal

Max H. Bazerman

The MIT Press
Cambridge, Massachusetts
London, England

The MIT Press
Massachusetts Institute of Technology
77 Massachusetts Avenue, Cambridge, MA 02139
mitpress.mit.edu

© 2025 Massachusetts Institute of Technology

All rights reserved. No part of this book may be used to train artificial intelligence systems or reproduced in any form by any electronic or mechanical means (including photocopying, recording, or information storage and retrieval) without permission in writing from the publisher.

The MIT Press would like to thank the anonymous peer reviewers who provided comments on drafts of this book. The generous work of academic experts is essential for establishing the authority and quality of our publications. We acknowledge with gratitude the contributions of these otherwise uncredited readers.

This book was set in ITC Stone Serif Std and ITC Stone Sans Std by New Best-set Typesetters Ltd. Printed and bound in the United States of America.

Library of Congress Cataloging-in-Publication Data

Names: Bazerman, Max H. author
Title: Inside an academic scandal : a story of fraud and betrayal / Max H. Bazerman, The MIT Press.
Description: Cambridge, Massachusetts : The MIT Press, [2025] | Includes bibliographical references and index.
Identifiers: LCCN 2024059962 (print) | LCCN 2024059963 (ebook) | ISBN 9780262049887 hardcover | ISBN 9780262384087 pdf | ISBN 9780262384094 epub
Subjects: LCSH: Cheating (Education)—United States | Academic writing—Moral and ethical aspects—United States | Harvard University—Graduate work | Universities and colleges—Corrupt practices—United States | Education, Higher—Moral and ethical aspects—United States
Classification: LCC LB3609 .B39 2026 (print) | LCC LB3609 (ebook) | DDC 378.1/98—dc23/eng/20250510
LC record available at https://lccn.loc.gov/2024059962
LC ebook record available at https://lccn.loc.gov/2024059963

10 9 8 7 6 5 4 3 2 1

EU Authorised Representative: Easy Access System Europe, Mustamäe tee 50, 10621 Tallinn, Estonia | Email: gpsr.requests@easproject.com

Dedicated to those with the courage to not be silent

# Contents

Preface   ix

1 "Your Paper Is Fraudulent"   1
2 Relationships and Trust   15
3 Crisis or Renaissance?   29
4 The Diffusion of Signing First   45
5 The Crisis   55
6 Accusations   69
7 The Lawsuit   79
8 The Fraudsters   89
9 Co-authors and Colleagues   101
10 Reactions and Repercussions   119
11 Why People Cheat   129
12 Moving Forward   145

Gratitude   159
Notes   161
Index   177

# Preface

Not long ago, my life was pleasant, interesting, and positively focused. I was (and still am) a tenured professor at the Harvard Business School. I loved teaching, whether my students were doctoral students, MBA students, or executives. I was well published and had received many international recognitions. I was free to write books based on my changing or evolving interests—and some of them even sold well. I enjoyed spending time with my many friends in academia, who were a pretty contented group themselves, despite the usual troubles we all run into in life. My biggest source of pride was my successful doctoral students, who hold great positions in many leading professional schools, including my own school. As 2019 drew to a close, hints of turbulence began to affect my satisfaction with my work and my life in general. But I had no idea of the changes that were about to unfold owing to my misguided pursuit of an interesting idea known as "signing first."

My early research, in the eighties and nineties, was in the areas of decision-making and negotiation. But for most of the current millennium, my work has focused more on behavioral ethics, or the psychology of how humans make moral decisions. My work is rooted in utilitarian philosophy, which assesses the ethicality of an action by asking whether it creates the most cumulative good possible. I try to do far more good than bad, and to make positive contributions to the world. I make decisions about what I teach, which consulting assignments I take, which research projects I embark on, which causes I donate money to, and what I eat (I'm a vegan) based on these values. Conducting research with integrity and studying topics connected to encouraging people to behave more ethically have been at the forefront of my mind for a long time. And throughout my entire career, I always assumed my co-authors had high ethical standards for their research as well.

In 2012, I was the fifth author of a paper published in a journal called *Proceedings of the National Academy of Sciences* that claimed to show that if a person agrees to tell the truth by signing their name *before* filling out a form (such as a tax form or an auto mileage reporting form), their responses will be more honest than if they sign such an honesty pledge in the traditional manner—that is, *after* filling out the form.[1] From 2018 to 2020, I took part in a research project that provided extensive evidence that this "signing-first" effect did not replicate—that is, that it did not hold up when tested repeatedly.[2] In 2020, I argued with the majority of my co-authors on the 2012 paper about whether we should retract our 2012 paper owing to lack of replicability of the findings. At that point, based on the decision of the majority of the co-authors, we did not retract the paper.

In 2021, a trio of academic bloggers known as Data Colada provided substantial evidence that one of the experiments described in the 2012 paper, an experiment that one of my co-authors claimed to have run, was fraudulent.[3] In 2023, Data Colada provided evidence that another experiment described in the same paper, led by a different co-author, was also fraudulent. The team's evidence was compelling. The media tried to cover the story, but the universities most closely connected to the alleged fraud were far from transparent. As a result of this opacity, the information on social and regular media about the scandal was often speculative, and in some cases wrong. Meanwhile, over one hundred co-authors of the alleged data fabricators had the rest of their work questioned, and the universities that employed my two co-authors whose work was in question began investigating them.

In 2022, I published a book titled *Complicit*, about people involved in allowing the wrongdoing of others. While I did not know that our paper was fraudulent until 2021, I had hints, and I had the opportunity to explore those hints in far greater detail than I did. If I had responded to these hints, all of which are documented in this book, I could have avoided being connected to this story of academic fraud. Like many people tangential to stories of wronging, I was complicit because of my failure to view the hints that I saw as warning signs worthy of attention.[4]

A few of my friends and colleagues raised the issue of how readers might interpret my motives for writing this book, including whether some might perceive the financial aspects of authorship to be a motive. While I reject that notion, I appreciate the insight into what others might think. With this concern in mind, I have committed to donating all of my advances and royalties from this book to the Scientific Integrity Fund (https://scientificintegrityfund.org/about-us).

I have been deeply affected by this story. It has reduced the joy I receive from academic pursuits, and it has damaged and demoralized my department, my school, and my field. I have also been frustrated by the incomplete and, at times, misleading coverage of the story in the media. This book is my effort to correct the record. I aim to be as transparent as possible about what occurred, to articulate remaining issues of concern about social science, and to offer suggestions for repairing the lost credibility of social science research.

**The Current Context**

This book is being published during a tough time for social science, and, more broadly, academia.

For the first time in my decades-long tenure as a professor, I am living under a U.S. president who seeks to harm universities, destroy their funding base, and limit their independence from the government. I strongly disagree with this political agenda, and side solidly with the universities who, in 2025, stood up for their principles, incurring substantial financial risk. Nothing that I document in this book is meant to criticize the enormous societal benefits of our university system. Rather, my critiques are part of a normal academic process to make our universities even stronger.

The purpose of this book is to document problems in the social sciences and provide insight about how universities can best promote honest, impactful research. I believe that the vast majority of social science research is honest, and honest researchers must be protected. I take pride in being transparent about what I see is in need of improvement. I am proud to be a university professor; our universities make enormous contributions to society.

There are forces exaggerating the claims about misconduct in the social sciences. At the same time, there are ethical, trustworthy scholars (documented in this book) working to improve social science research. The former are not helpful; the latter are moving the field forward. It is in this context that I offer my insider's perspective on a visible scandal in social science. My goal is to make research better.

A point worth repeating: I am opposed to those who exaggerate what's wrong with academia and actively oppose those seeking to harm American universities. When governments withdraw research funding, we all lose.

# 1 "Your Paper Is Fraudulent"

On July 15, 2021, my co-authors Lisa Shu, Nina Mazar, Francesca Gino, Dan Ariely, and I received an email from researchers and "data detectives" Leif Nelson, Joe Simmons, and Uri Simonsohn informing us they had compelling evidence that our well-cited 2012 research paper, "Signing at the Beginning Makes Ethics Salient and Decreases Dishonest Self-Reports in Comparison to Signing at the End" (known as the "signing-first" paper), was fraudulent.[1] The paper claimed to show that you could increase people's honesty by simply having them sign a promise to tell the truth *before* filling out a form, rather than after, as is traditionally done. Nelson, Simmons, and Simonsohn planned to go public with this news on Data Colada, their well-respected academic blog.[2] They offered us an advance look at the blog post, "Evidence of Fraud in an Influential Field Experiment About Dishonesty,"[3] and an opportunity to respond.

The email was not a surprise to me. Nelson, a professor at the University of California at Berkeley's business school, had requested a Zoom meeting with me three weeks earlier to discuss "a fairly serious topic," as he put it. Nelson wrote in his email to me, "We are coming to you as someone who can offer us sage advice and as someone who is in a position to help."

As I faced the three members of Data Colada in separate Zoom boxes, I had no idea what was up. They explained that they had found problems with Study 3, one of the three research experiments described in the signing-first paper. They had found compelling evidence that the data in this field experiment, ostensibly obtained from an insurance company, were highly problematic, they told me. One of my co-authors on the paper, Duke professor Dan Ariely, had been the point person with the insurance company and had provided the rest of us with the data. By the end of the Zoom call, Data Colada had overviewed the irregularities in the data for the insurance study and convinced me that Ariely's insurance data were fraudulent. The idea that I had co-published a paper based on fraudulent data was, to say the least, shocking and upsetting. It was a possibility I had never considered during my long academic career.

And there was more. On the same Zoom call, the Data Colada team laid out evidence suggesting that Study 1 in the same paper, a lab experiment, was also fraudulent. As the Data Colada team already knew, another co-author on the study, Francesca Gino—my friend, former advisee, frequent co-author, and colleague at the Harvard Business School—had managed all aspects of the data in Study 1 of the signing-first paper. Then the news got even worse: Data Colada had investigated other papers co-authored by Gino and uncovered evidence of data fraud in three more of them (none of which I was involved in). The pattern of data fabrication, they alleged, was similar across all four papers. Nelson, Simmons, and Simonsohn felt that Gino's employer (and mine), Harvard University, should be informed of the results of their investigation into Gino's work. We discussed whom they might speak to at the university.

Data Colada was planning to publicly post the evidence of data fraud in Study 3, the study that Ariely had been responsible for. But, for reasons not provided to me, they preferred to give the evidence on Study 1 and Gino's other three concerning papers to Harvard. Within a few weeks, I'd heard from multiple Harvard administrators. Their advice was consistent: It was important to keep Data Colada's allegations about Study 1 under wraps. Failing to do so, they told me, could interfere with a possible investigation of Gino.

It was time for me to prepare my public response to Data Colada's impending blog post about Study 3. While I was not responsible for the data, my name was on the paper—a widely cited one that had been published in a reputable academic journal almost a decade earlier. I sent my public response to the appropriate Harvard administrators for their review. They encouraged me to shorten my response and recommended that I delete three sentences that alluded to my suspicions about Study 1. I deleted the sentences. The Data Colada team went public with their evidence of data fabrication in Study 3 on August 17, 2021, about a month after their initial email to me and my four co-authors about the signing-first paper.

From July 2021, when Harvard learned of Gino's alleged data fabrication, until June 2023, nearly two years later, no one from Harvard (university administrators, my dean, lawyers, investigators, etc.) interviewed me, nor did anyone update me on the investigation. For nearly two years, I assumed the Gino investigation would be completed soon.

A few media outlets covered the Data Colada Study 3 fraud post, focusing on Dan Ariely. And in November 2022, I published my book *Complicit: How We Enable the Unethical and How to Stop*, which included a chapter on the Study 3 insurance study with only a passing mention of Study 1, even though I was fully aware that Study 1 likely was also based on fabricated data. Harvard was still investigating.

Then, in June 2023, nearly two years after their shocking Zoom call with me, Data Colada published detailed evidence on their blog that Study 1 of our signing-first paper, as well as three other papers co-authored by Gino, was fraudulent. They also noted that Harvard had placed Gino on administrative leave and that this information was publicly available on Gino's HBS website. "We believe that many more Gino-authored papers contain fake data," Data Colada wrote. "Perhaps dozens."

This time, the story was reported widely in the press. The devastating impact this news had on our field cannot be overstated. Gino was a prolific researcher; she'd published 135 papers with 148 co-authors and had written two popular trade books. Her co-authors were understandably horrified (as I had been) to learn that their research could very well be based on fabricated data. In many of these studies, Gino had complete control of the data. She was also a well-liked colleague, a friend to many. Those of us who thought we knew her well were left reeling. If someone we trusted had repeatedly, and apparently easily, allegedly committed fraud over the course of her career, what did this say about our research and, indeed, about social science?

Gino's co-authors were left with the task of figuring out whether they should trust their own published work, what to tell their own universities, and whether to retract their published papers. At least one co-author had a prestigious award revoked since it was based on work she'd co-authored with Gino. Organizations and at least one national government had invested substantial resources implementing the results of the signing-first paper. The journal *Science* reported that a research group led by Michael Sanders had spent $250,000 running an experiment on tax compliance in Guatemala based on the effects of the signing-first paper—an experiment that (unsurprisingly) didn't work. Sanders reported his efforts were wasted "because we were digging in the wrong place."[4] Science deniers used this study as one more reason not to trust science.

## A Bit About Me

This book is the story of one of the most significant academic scandals of our time. I offer an inside look at how such extensive fraud could occur in academia generally and at Harvard specifically. Because I was close to many of the people involved and a co-author of eight empirical papers with Francesca Gino, you should know more about me as you consider my presentation of this story.

The events of 2021 broke soon before my sixty-sixth birthday. I am a tenured professor at Harvard, have published a couple hundred papers and fourteen books (before this one), and take pride in my role as an adviser to dozens of doctoral students. Many of my advisees, including Dolly Chugh, Katy Milkman, Don Moore, and Todd Rogers, are among the best-known scholars in the field. My doctoral students have accepted positions at leading business schools throughout the United States, including the Kellogg School of Management at Northwestern University, the Wharton School at the University of Pennsylvania, the Fuqua School of Business at Duke University, the Haas School of Business at the University of California at Berkeley, the S. C. Johnson Graduate School of Management at Cornell University, Carnegie Mellon University, Stanford University, the University of Chicago, the University of Notre Dame, Columbia University, and HBS. These advisees are among the most important people in my life.

I love academic research and believe that it helps make the world a better place. I apply what I learn in the research process to advise corporations and governments on how to make better decisions. My consulting, teaching, and lecturing have taken me to thirty-two countries over the course of my forty-five-year career. I say no to projects that I do not believe will contribute to making the world a better place. I am well recognized for my work, having received an honorary doctorate from the University of London (London Business School), the Life Achievement Award from the Aspen Institute, and both the Distinguished Scholar Award and the Distinguished Educator Award from the Academy of Management.

I have also been recognized on the ethics front, having been named one of Ethisphere's "100 Most Influential people in Business Ethics" and a Daily

Kos Hero for going public about how the Bush administration corrupted the RICO tobacco trial.[5] The latter recognition came for speaking up publicly when I was an expert witness for the U.S. Department of Justice and accused Robert McCallum, then the associate attorney general, of interfering with the government's prosecution of the tobacco industry.[6] This accusation provided me with a reputation for being willing to speak up in the face of wrongdoing.

As noted in the preface, most of my early research centered on decision-making and negotiation, namely, on the systematic mistakes we make and how we can do better. In the current millennium, I have focused more on topics in the field of behavioral ethics, which explores the psychology of how we make ethical decisions. Since 2011, I have published three books on ethics: *Blind Spots: Why We Fail to Do What's Right and What to Do About It* (with Ann Tenbrunsel), *Better, Not Perfect: A Realist's Guide to Maximum Sustainable Goodness*, and *Complicit: How We Enable the Unethical and How to Stop*. In this book, I will draw on ideas from these books to help explain why researchers in my field engaged in fraud and why so many scholars, including me, allowed this scandal to occur and go unrecognized for a decade. In my effort to understand what happened during and after the publication of the fraudulent signing-first paper, I will apply current research on why people engage in unethical behavior and how we can encourage more ethical behavior in ourselves and others.

## The Insurance Company Study—as I Knew It—in 2012

Our 2012 signing-first paper was central to uncovering allegations against Francesca Gino. But media coverage of the story started with evidence of data fabrication in the insurance study of the paper—data that Dan Ariely brought to our five-author team. The signing-first paper was part of a fairly recent movement in social science to identify simple "nudges" to get people to behave more consistently in line with their and society's best interests—including, in the case of our paper, to coax people to make more ethical decisions.

As mentioned earlier, in our signing-first paper we claimed, based on our research results, that if an organization asked people to sign a statement promising to tell the truth *before* they filled out a form, they would provide more honest information than if they signed such a statement *after* providing the requested information. Imagine signing a request for reimbursement or your tax form. The idea that signing before you report this information might encourage you to be more honest seemed intuitively and theoretically possible. It's also an appealing idea, since it would offer an easy pathway for driving more ethical behavior. When we wrote our 2012 paper, we focused on paper-and-pencil forms. But, as I'll explain later in the book, the issue of filling out forms online raises some interesting new issues—and ends up being core to the story I'm telling.

The signing-first paper combined two empirical efforts, neither of which had yet been published. Lisa Shu (a Harvard PhD student at the time), Gino, and I claimed to have evidence from two laboratory experiments conducted at the University of North Carolina (Gino's employer before she joined HBS) that signing first improves honesty. We claimed that in two lab studies, participants were asked at the end of the experiment to self-report how much money they had earned by correctly solving puzzles. Participants were paid according to their self-reports. They were asked to provide a signature to verify the honesty of their reporting *before* reporting the amount they had earned (signing first) or *after* reporting the amount they had earned (signing after). Unbeknown to the participants, we knew exactly how much they had earned in the experiment; this information allowed us to assess whether they overreported their earnings—that is, whether they cheated. We reported that participants cheated significantly less often when they signed at the top of the reporting form than when they signed at the bottom of the form.

Gino, Shu, and I wrote up our paper and sent it to multiple journals for review. It was rejected for publication, and the feedback we received led us to believe that supporting our lab studies with field evidence would make our paper more convincing. Ariely, meanwhile, had presented evidence in multiple forums of the same effect from a field experiment allegedly conducted at an insurance company starting in 2008. All three of us knew about the field evidence on signing first that Ariely had presented but not published. Ariely and Gino were friends, had published prior papers together, and worked ten miles away from each other when Gino taught at the University of North Carolina and Ariely taught at Duke. So Gino contacted Ariely in January of 2011 about the idea of combining efforts.

Ariely responded positively and added that he had been working on this research project with Nina Mazar, so she would need to be involved as well.

Mazar, now a professor at Boston University, was then on the faculty of the University of Toronto and had previously been a postdoctoral associate of Ariely. She and Ariely were also among the co-founders of the behavioral science consulting firm BEworks, Inc. So Gino emailed Mazar, who also was game to team up: "It's a good idea to combine forces," she wrote. (A decade later, after we had all received Data Colada's 2021 email alleging fraud, Mazar made clear in an email to me that her prior collaboration with Ariely on the topic was limited to mentioning the idea of "signing first" in a prior publication of theirs; the two of them had not been working on the topic before Gino reached out to Ariely, she explained. Given Ariely's response, however, I had assumed that Mazar was involved in the field experiment.)

The two research projects—the Shu-Gino-Bazerman experiment and the Ariely-led insurance experiment—were synergistic, each responding to limitations of the other. The Shu-Gino-Bazerman studies claimed to provide precisely controlled laboratory experiments. Ariely's insurance study claimed to provide a field experiment using data from an actual insurance company.

In the insurance study, Ariely claimed that the insurance company's customers were randomly assigned to sign an honesty statement either before or after reporting mileage from their car's odometer—that is, at either the top or the bottom of the form. The insurance company charged customers more if they drove more. So some customers could deduce that they could save money by unethically underreporting their mileage. According to Ariely, data were collected from customers at two points in time. The first point was before Ariely or other researchers were involved; presumably, all customers in the study had received the same form to fill out at this first point in time. At the second point in time, according to Ariely, customers were randomly assigned to one of two conditions—signing *before* or signing *after*.

Note that there is no reason that odometer readings reported at the first measurement would differ significantly between the two conditions since customers had not yet been assigned to a condition. For the second odometer reading, the prediction was that signing before reporting mileage would lead customers to report more honestly than if they signed after reporting. The core measure for the study was the difference between the mileage reports at time 1 and time 2, or the number of miles customers claimed to have driven between those two points in time. Randomly assigning customers to the two conditions for time 2 created an experiment, such that any difference in mileage reporting could be causally explained based on when they signed the form (before or after reporting mileage).

Unknown to me at the time, Ariely sent an Excel file with the alleged insurance company data to Nina Mazar. She reported to Ariely, but not to me or, I assume, to the other co-authors on the project, that the results pointed in the wrong direction: In fact, people who had signed at the top of the form were *less* honest than those who had signed at the bottom, according to a September 2023 *New Yorker* article about the scandal.[7] Ariely responded to Mazar that in making "the dataset nicer" for her, he had relabeled the conditions accidentally, and he asked her to switch them back. "The metadata for the Excel file that [Ariely] sent to Mazar note that it was created, and last edited, by a user named Dan Ariely," according to the *New Yorker*. Given the bond between Ariely and Mazar, I can completely understand Mazar's trust in Ariely's explanations during this peculiar episode regarding the insurance data.

By the end of February 2011, I had first received a draft of a paper that included all three studies, with no knowledge of the exchange between Ariely and Mazar. Gino, Shu, and Mazar had written and edited the paper. This was the first time I read it, including details about the insurance company. In this draft, Study 3 reported that customers who signed *after* reporting their odometer mileage had driven 23,601 miles in the past year and customers who signed *before* reporting their mileage had driven 26,098 miles in the past year. That is, moving the signature from the bottom to the top of the form seemed to reduce underreporting by 2,497 miles. This was a huge, statistically significant difference between conditions—large enough, in retrospect, that it should have raised suspicions. Could Ariely really have found such a huge effect by simply moving the signature line?

Over my long career, I had never questioned the integrity of a co-author, and I didn't then, either. My collaborations were always based on trust. Besides, I liked the core idea that all three studies seemed to confirm: that attesting to their honesty before reporting led people to consider the ethical dimension of what they were about to report, which made them more honest.

While I wasn't thinking about fraud, I was nervous about what I read in Study 3. Specifically, I found it strange that customers had driven such a large number of miles in one year in both conditions—averaging over

24,000 miles. "The means for the number of miles driven in a year seem enormous—twice what I would have expected," I emailed my co-authors in March 2011. "Am I simply wrong, is the sample unusual, or is there an error in recording the data?" Ariely responded to me quickly with a brief email: "the milage [sic] are correct." I found his lack of attention to my critique annoying, as I was simply trying to check our methods. I spoke with Gino and Shu multiple times at Harvard, reiterating my concerns about the insurance company data—specifically, the high number of miles driven—and about Ariely dismissing my question.

After I kept pushing for information, Ariely sent an email to me and our other co-authors in April 2011 that read: "We used an older population mostly in Florida—but we can't tell how we got the data, who was the population (they were all AARP members)—and we also can't show the forms." This did not address why the customers' mileage would be so high. In fact, if an elderly population had formed the study group, this would suggest the miles driven would have been even lower. As 2011 progressed, I still didn't have answers to my questions about the insurance study.

In January 2012, I flew to San Diego to speak at the annual meeting of the Society for Personality and Social Psychology. The day I arrived, in a large and busy hallway, I ran into Lisa Shu, who was with Nina Mazar, whom I'd never met. After Lisa introduced us, we sat down at a round table, and I expressed my frustration with Ariely's seeming inability to explain the mileage issue. I wanted to believe that the signing-first effect was real, but was really annoyed by that point that he hadn't explained the data clearly. Mazar calmly pulled out her laptop and opened the data file that we were discussing. We were simply dealing with a minor issue regarding how the data were explained in the paper, she said. The confusion came from the first odometer reading, she explained. She clarified that our paper, which had been submitted to two different academic journals, was wrong in stating that the number of miles reported had been driven in a year, when in fact we didn't know when the first odometer readings had been taken. She suggested that probably more than a year had passed between the first and second odometer readings.

I received no explanation for why Mazar and Ariely had not clarified this point earlier. Mazar's explanation of the data was plausible, and I was relieved. I completely trust that Mazar had good intentions as she clarified the data to me. Obviously, we needed to edit the paper so that our presentation of our research methods was accurate. Unfortunately, not knowing when the first measure was taken would make the experiment less precise, but if the customers were randomly assigned for the second measurement, an experiment was still in effect. It still didn't occur to me that the data Mazar received from Ariely, which Ariely claimed he had received from the insurance company, might be fraudulent.

As I tried to understand the data, I received confusing messages from Ariely. After receiving one of these messages, I sent an email in March 2012 to only Shu and Gino, my colleagues at Harvard: "I have read this carefully, and remain uncomfortable with our understanding of the data. . . . I am happy to withdraw [from the paper], and make no bad inferences based on what you choose to do. See you both soon, Max." Later that evening, I sent another email to Shu and Gino: "I recommend taking our studies back, invited [sic] Nina [Mazar] to join us, and running away from the auto data. Alternatively, I am happy to simply withdraw. Max." I received multiple communications from Shu and Gino saying that Mazar had made them comfortable with the validity of the data. I failed to follow through on withdrawing from the project owing to my concern about how doing so would affect Shu, who was on the academic job market at the time and had presented this work with my name attached.

In my quest to better understand confusing data, I had asked many questions, but not enough of them. I also didn't verify the work of others. When I met Mazar in person, I didn't ask her why she hadn't responded to my questions in the many emails I'd sent to our team throughout 2011, if she had answers readily available. It wasn't until 2021, when the story of fraud broke, that I learned I had had access to the insurance company data: On May 26, 2012, Mazar uploaded this data file to Dropbox and told all the co-authors via email that it was there. I didn't pay attention to this email as my frustration with the project had increased to the point that I didn't want to think about it. In 2021, Simonsohn and multiple co-authors of the 2012 paper made me aware of my access. This failure to check data provided by my co-authors was not unusual for me. As has been true for many of my other published papers, I trusted others, and the thought that I might need to verify the integrity of colleagues never crossed my mind. I was not the only member of the co-author group who was too trusting, either. Other co-authors too readily accepted explanations for peculiarities in our field data. I will return to this theme in discussing the role of co-authors in chapter 12.

## The Rest of the Story

In this book, I take you on a journey that describes what happened after our paper was published in 2012. I explain how the ideas presented in our signing-first paper diffused to organizations and governments. I introduce you to my distant cousin, Stu Baserman, an insurtech founder, who hired me to offer advice on how to get insurance claimants to tell the truth online. Stu's interest led me to start a research project, beyond the insurance industry, aimed at getting people to tell the truth online. This project brought in Ariella Kristal (then a PhD student at Harvard) and Ashley Whillans (then an assistant professor in the same department as Gino and me), who led the research efforts showing that the signing-first effect did not replicate. Kristal, Whillans, myself, and the four other original authors of the signing-first paper (Ariely, Gino, Mazar, and Shu) published a paper in 2020 that included seven experiments that showed strong evidence that the signing-first effect did not replicate. This paper was published despite multiple co-authors throwing up many barriers.

The story continues through 2021, when Data Colada first discovered fraudulent data in the insurance study and in several other publications that Gino had co-authored. I'll describe my shock at discovering that a close, trusted colleague was accused of committing fraud throughout much of her career, while I advised her and worked with her. I explore what did and didn't happen in 2021, after the evidence of her fraud emerged, as well as the nearly two years of silence that followed. I continue the story as the fraud unfolded in the press in 2023 and 2024. A timeline follows at the end of the chapter to help provide an overview of key events in this story.

While I hope to tell a compelling story, my broader aim is for this story to serve as a vehicle for improving the integrity of social science. I will frame this specific story of data fabrication within the movement for social science reform that has sprung up over the last fifteen years. We will consider how other instances of fraud motivated these efforts and why data fabrication continues to occur. We will review the psychology behind dishonest behavior, as well as why those of us who find ourselves in proximity to fraud often fail to take steps to stop it. Finally, I will offer insight into further changes that are needed from researchers, universities, academic journals, and research funders to create credible and believable social science that can make the world better.

**2003**

I receive my first email from Francesca Gino.

**2004**

I meet Gino and start working with her on projects.

**2007**

Dan Ariely presents the insurance study (later published as Study 3 of the "signing-first" paper) in public forums.

**2010**

Gino joins the Harvard Business School faculty.

Marc Hauser resigns from Harvard University amid allegations of data fabrication.

**2011**

Lisa Shu, Gino, and I combine two lab experiments with the insurance field experiment from Ariely (with some role from Mazar) into the first draft of the signing-first paper.

I raise multiple questions about the data in the insurance study.

The Data Colada team publish their paper on p-hacking, which creates a stir.

Diederik Stapel resigns from Tilburg University amid allegations of data fabrication.

**2012**

Mazar provides viable explanations for the idiosyncrasies I observed in the insurance study data.

Shu, Mazar, Gino, Ariely, and Bazerman publish the signing-first paper in *PNAS*.

**2016**

I meet Stuart Baserman of Slice Insurance and become intrigued with the idea of how to get people to tell the truth online.

**2017**

I initiate a project with Ariella Kristal and Ashley Whillans on how to get people to tell the truth online, starting with the idea of having them sign first. For the next two years, we repeatedly fail to replicate the effect.

**Figure 1.1**
Timeline of an academic scandal.

**2018**

Kristal, Whillans, and I invite Shu, Mazar, Gino and Ariely to join the replication project, which includes rerunning one of the original studies with a much larger sample size. All agree to join.

**2019**

A massive replication of the signing-first project again fails. Significant conflict arises between myself and other co-authors about how to report the failure to replicate.

**2020**

The signing-first co-authors argue repeatedly about the validity of the signing-first result and how to present our failures to replicate.

We publish the evidence on the failure to replicate in *PNAS*.

The co-authors dispute whether to retract the 2012 paper. The majority vote against retraction.

**2021**

Data Colada posts strong evidence suggesting that the insurance study in the 2012 signing-first paper is fraudulent.

Data Colada provides Harvard University with allegations that Study 1 from the signing-first paper, as well as three other studies co-authored by Gino, are fraudulent.

**2022**

I learn that Harvard is investigating Gino, but the university remains silent on the matter.

I publish *Complicit: How We Enable the Unethical and How to Stop*, which tells the story of Study 3 in the signing-first paper but not Study 1.

**2023**

Harvard University places Gino on administrative leave of absence without pay.

Data Colada publishes evidence alleging fraud in four different papers co-authored by Gino.

Gino sues Harvard University and Data Colada for $25 million.

**2024**

The judge in the lawsuit filed by Gino makes Harvard's 1,254 page report on Gino's alleged fraud public.

The judge grants Harvard's and Data Colada's motions to dismiss the defamation charges while allowing the breach of contract claim against Harvard to move forward.

**Figure 1.1 (continued)**

Throughout my career, I have studied foibles and biases in human behavior in an effort to find ways that we can all make better decisions and behave in greater harmony with our ethics. In this book, I take a close look at the fraud of those around me, as well as at my own complicity in their fraud. This experience has been devastating to me and to many other social science researchers. But I believe that, as in the past, there are lessons we can glean from unethical behavior to prevent it from repeating. I will try to identify such lessons and, in the process, find some good amid this upsetting episode.

# 2 Relationships and Trust

Relationships and trust are at the center of this data fabrication story. For many academics, our closest friends are often our colleagues, co-authors, advisers, and students. This certainly has been the case for me. We spend time together in offices, classrooms, and conference rooms discussing and debating ideas, brainstorming interesting research projects, and teaching and learning from each other. We socialize at conferences, celebrate each other's career achievements and life milestones, and catch up over coffee and lunch. Some of my colleagues have become my best friends—people I always look forward to spending time with.

Aside from the rewards of friendship and camaraderie, being able to trust our colleagues creates enormous opportunities in academic careers. Trust allows researchers to be much more efficient when creating new knowledge. We can achieve so much more when we trust the work of others, rather than needing to closely monitor or redo what they have done. Trust also helps us build and cement relationships; we like people who trust us, and we like people who seem trustworthy. And it's simply easier to trust our colleagues: Asking to check their data could easily sound like an accusation and could even end up threatening the relationship.

Organizational scholars Roger Meyer, Jim Davis, and David Schoorman distinguish between three different bases of trust: ability, benevolence, and integrity.[1] When you say "I trust you," you could be commenting on someone's perceived competence to complete a task (ability), their generosity (benevolence), or their intention to do what they say (integrity). In the course of my work, I can easily recall using the term "trust" to refer to my trust in colleagues' ability and benevolence. Prior to the scandal described here, I have had concerns about co-authors' ability to complete a task. I have certainly observed conflicts among academics about giving credit for work performed (lack of benevolence). But before I worked on the signing-first paper, I never questioned the integrity of someone in my research group. I believe that until recently, most of us who work in social science labs implicitly trusted the integrity of our colleagues.

My understanding of trust allows me to examine and reflect on the relationships and resulting trust among the parties in the signing-first story. In this chapter, I introduce the key characters in the story, explain how they are connected, and describe how these relationships enabled the fabrication of data to occur and go undetected for years.

**Francesca Gino**

On May 12, 2003, I received my first email from Francesca Gino:

Dear Max,

I've been sitting in the NOM talks for the last few weeks, and I'd like to be added in the mailing list for the seminars you mentioned this afternoon.

I'm a visiting fellow at HBS/Harvard University for the current year and I've been re-admitted for next year as well. So, I'll be happy to join the seminars and talks that will be offered next year.

Many thanks.
Francesca (Gino)

NOM stands for the Negotiation, Organizations and Markets unit, my department at HBS. Like many academic departments, we host regular research presentations. Francesca was then a second-year PhD student in economics and management at the Sant'Anna School of Advanced Studies in Pisa, Italy, and, as she mentioned, a visiting fellow at HBS. In an email response, I welcomed Francesca to attend the talks, and I asked a colleague to add her to the email list to receive notices about future seminars that might be of interest to her.

Francesca began attending the talks, and by early 2004, I was interacting regularly with her. She struck me as pleasant, resilient to tough feedback, and hard-working, and I enjoyed our meetings. She visited Italy often but began attending my doctoral seminar in the spring of 2004 when she was in the Boston-Cambridge area. The doctoral seminar was an HBS course with about fifteen to twenty students, primarily doctoral students from around Harvard University. I offered comments on her dissertation research, which included work on advice taking, and eventually I served on her dissertation committee. We also started working on a research project together that focused on the slippery slope of unethical behavior—the tendency for people's ethical behavior to degrade slowly over time rather than all at once; this work was eventually published in 2009.[2] By the spring of 2004, Francesca had accepted an offer for a postdoctoral position (a "postdoc," in academic jargon) at HBS for two years, 2004–2006. I was not involved in the decision to offer this position.

Francesca became a regular member of my lab group. The lab group was a regular gathering of doctoral students working on research in the general areas that I studied: ethics, decision-making, and negotiation. Since one of the topics of Francesca's dissertation research was advice taking, in 2004, I introduced her to an advisee, friend, and co-author of mine who had also studied advice: Don Moore, who was then on the faculty at Carnegie Mellon University. Don is a generous person who I expected would take the time to interact with this visiting doctoral student. Eventually, Don and Francesca formed a research collaboration and friendship. Don has gone on to be a central figure in the open science movement, which has emerged to strengthen the integrity of scientific research, in addition to serving as a professor, academic dean, and acting dean of the Haas School of Business at UC Berkeley.

The research on advice taking generally shows that people underuse advice from others. A common method in advice-taking experiments is for a study participant to be asked to estimate some quantity, such as the year in which some historic event took place, the weight of a person or a big fish in a photo, or the market capitalization of a specified corporation. The participant would then get advice from someone else about the same quantity, and the participant would then have a chance to revise their initial estimate. Revised estimates tend to be more accurate, yet participants tend to underweight advice from others and overweight their own opinions when making decisions.

A common metric in advice-taking studies is weight-on-advice (WOA), or the weight we assign to the advice of another party. Imagine that you estimate the weight of someone in a photo to be 150 pounds. You then find out that another study participant estimated the person's weight to be 160 pounds. You are given an opportunity to revise your estimate, and you know that you will be financially rewarded based on the accuracy of your assessment. If you completely ignore the other participant's advice and stick with your estimate of 150 pounds, the WOA would be 0, reflecting full discounting of the other participant's advice. If you changed your answer to 160, your WOA would be 1.0, reflecting complete acceptance of the advice. If you went with 153, your WOA would be .3. In these studies, it is very rare for participants' second estimates to fall outside the two initial estimates (150–160, in this case).

When I started drafting this chapter, I reviewed hundreds of emails to, from, and related to my co-authors on the signing-first study. I was surprised to come across an email I had sent to Francesca on July 4, 2004, in which I commented on the advice-taking study in her dissertation. "If I understand your reporting," I wrote to her, "11% of your observations are outside the range between the subject and the adviser. Why? My impression from [another doctoral student who studied advice taking] is that this [is] rare. Can you review your data and see what is going on here?" I never received a response, and I don't think I thought about the issue again. Despite the unusual data, I never considered the possibility of data fabrication. Rather, I simply saw a quirk in something that a junior colleague sent me.

By the spring of 2006, Francesca was confident she would receive an offer to join the HBS faculty in the Technology and Operations Management area. That offer did not come through, leaving her without clear plans for the future, as her postdoc ended in the summer of 2006. I recommended Francesca in an email to Don Moore, and Carnegie Mellon soon hired her for a two-year visiting assistant professor position. My understanding is that Don was supportive of hiring Francesca but did not dominate the decision-making process that led Francesca to be hired.

I continued to read Francesca's published work during her two years at Carnegie Mellon, which she followed with two years in a tenure-track faculty position at the University of North Carolina (from summer 2008 to summer 2010). In 2007, Lisa Shu joined the organizational behavior doctoral program at Harvard. By early 2008, Francesca, Lisa, and I had begun working on a number of research studies together. By the end of 2008, we had a multistudy paper under review at a journal that would be published in 2011 as "Dishonest Deed, Clear Conscience: When Cheating Leads to Moral Disengagement and Motivated Forgetting."[3] In March 2009, I visited UNC to present my research, and Francesca served as my primary host, organizing my activities. I recall having a fantastic breakfast meeting on that trip, mainly about mentorship in academia, with psychologist Adam Grant, before he became famous—he was then a productive assistant professor at UNC, like Francesca. That June, I was one of four American academics who traveled to Tione, Italy, to attend Francesca's wedding to Greg Burd. Don Moore was one of the three others.

On November 24, 2009, I sent Francesca an email asking her to send me the papers she had written on the behavioral aspects of ethics for a book I was writing with Notre Dame professor Ann Tenbrunsel, my former mentee, about bounded ethicality—the ways in which good people act unethically without their own awareness. "You seem to create published stuff on behavioral aspects of ethics faster than anyone around," I noted to Francesca, adding, "I realize that this is a lot of papers. I promise to read them all!" Within two hours, fifteen papers from Francesca had arrived in my inbox. This was an astounding number of papers for someone who had been a professor for only a couple of years.

By the summer of 2010, Francesca had come back to HBS, joining my unit (NOM) as a tenure-track faculty member. I was delighted to have my friend and colleague join our group. Francesca had a positive, enthusiastic style that many at HBS valued and that attracted lots of co-authors. I continued to develop new research projects with her on topics related to ethics even as she produced published research with others at a remarkable pace.

By early 2011, the five authors of the 2012 signing-first paper had joined forces. In June of that year, I was in a car with my spouse, Marla, and our fifteen-year-old dog, Timber, heading across the country for a sabbatical at UC Berkeley, where Don Moore was then teaching. Though the sabbatical was only for a year, Marla and I were thinking about staying in Berkeley for the rest of our lives. I had good indications that the Haas School of Business at Berkeley would be interested in making me a tenured job offer. We were looking forward to the natural beauty, mild weather, great vegetarian food, and proximity to our preferred beverage—Napa Valley cabernets. But after a short time in Berkeley, we realized we missed our life in Cambridge.

Much of the email dialogue among the five co-authors on the signing-first paper occurred while I was in Berkeley during the 2011–12 academic year. That year, I made regular trips back to Cambridge for executive teaching, meetings with doctoral students, and some personnel matters. On many of my visits, Francesca and Greg hosted a wonderful dinner at their Harvard-owned three-bedroom apartment in Cambridge, which featured

Francesca's Italian cooking and an assembly of some of my favorite people at Harvard. (Harvard gives faculty the option of renting apartments that it owns.) Being geeks, we talked about academic matters, including, at one dinner, outlining an organization that would become the Behavioral Insights Group at Harvard, with Iris Bohnet and myself as the co-leaders. These dinners were an important reminder of what I loved about my life at Harvard—the camaraderie, interesting conversations, and sense of being among trusted, lifelong friends. I appreciated Francesca's generosity in hosting these gatherings, which she said were part of her recruiting strategy to make sure I returned to Harvard from my sabbatical.

Marla, Timber (now sixteen), and I made plans to return to what we now thought of as "home" in May 2012, but we had trouble finding a home to buy in Cambridge while we were still in Berkeley. As we drove out of California, we still had no place to live in Massachusetts. But Francesca and Greg were spending six weeks in London, and they generously offered their Cambridge house for Marla, Timber, and me to live in for free. So we simply moved into the Gino-Burd home during this time, though we insisted on paying the rent.

Over the next few years, my relationship with Francesca was excellent—one of close, trusted colleagues and friends: We wrote papers together, taught in the same executive programs, and socialized together. With our spouses, we even considered jointly buying into a condo development project so that we could build homes next to each other—that's how much we enjoyed each other's company and trusted one another.

In a YouTube video posted in 2015, Francesca described my influence on her and her career:[4]

> I've had the privilege of having so many wonderful teachers both in the United States and back in Italy. One of them who was pretty remarkable is Max Bazerman, who's a professor at Harvard Business School and now a dear colleague of mine. He is special in three main ways. First, he is incredibly curious, and he triggers and encourages a lot of curiosity in all of his students. So I remember taking one of his classes when I visited Harvard, and he would keep asking you to think about what the scholar wanted to say, or when you asked a question, he turned it around and had a question for you: What do you think this author is trying to say, or how is it that the paper could have been written differently? Second, he is a person who is able to give you tough feedback, and he's willing to do that even if the feedback is hard to give. And I remember one time being in his office, and he was smiling, telling me something very critical that I needed to hear, and

then he ended by saying, I know that you can take the hard feedback. I left his office and I was crying, but it was so critical to my development as a scholar. And finally, Max is an amazing person, not only a great scholar. Every time I face a tough decision, I can hear myself asking, what would Max do in this situation? So, a wonderful teacher, one that made a real difference in my life, and in fact it was the main reason why I decided after my visit to Harvard Business School to stay and try to find a career and a job here rather than going back to Italy.

In 2015, the website Poets and Quants, which reports on business schools, included Francesca in its list of "Best 40 under 40" B-school professors. Asked which professor she most admired, she named me, for always inspiring her to "be a better scholar and a better human being." I took pride in watching Francesca succeed. As colleagues, she and I jointly advised other doctoral students, including Ting Zhang (now a professor at HBS) and Ovul Sezer (now a professor at Cornell).

Francesca's reputation was soaring, both in academia and in the consulting world. In 2016, she was appointed editor of a leading journal, *Organizational Behavior and Human Decision Processes*, and in 2018 she became the unit head of our HBS academic department, thus becoming my boss. During this time, my perception was that Francesca was overcommitted to executive teaching, consulting, research, book writing, and other obligations. We had multiple conflicts over decisions within the NOM unit, and our relationship started to deteriorate by the end of the decade. It became clear to me that Francesca no longer found my input on the management of our unit helpful, and our social gatherings were less frequent. In 2021, citing overcommitment, in part from raising four children during the COVID-19 pandemic, Francesca stepped down from her position as unit head, remaining a tenured member of the unit.

**Lisa Shu**

I met Lisa Shu in the spring of 2005 when she joined my doctoral seminar, "Behavioral Aspects of Decision Making and Negotiation"—the same seminar that Francesca had attended a year earlier. Lisa was a junior at Harvard, double majoring in psychology and economics. She was part of Dan Gilbert's lab group in the psychology department, and I was amazed by her early intellectual sophistication: Among the PhD students in the seminar, she more than held her own. Harvard undergrads live in "houses" rather than dorms, and Lisa lived in Leverett House. Students are given the opportunity to invite a professor to a student-faculty dinner, and Lisa invited me to attend as her guest at Leverett House on March 23, 2005. I was happy to attend.

Students were required to work on developing a research proposal as part of my class. Lisa worked on a project on the endowment effect—the tendency to value items we own more highly than we would if we did not own them. This tendency can lead sellers to charge too much and for their item to go unsold, as in the case of a home seller whose listing price is more than the market will bear. Gilbert was Lisa's main adviser, but I spent a fair amount of time advising her on her experimental designs for the project. I enjoyed our interactions. Her proposal led to her senior thesis, which received numerous awards from the psychology and economics departments.[5]

When Lisa graduated from Harvard in 2006, she sent me an email to update me on her plans for the year. This included "writing for Let's Go travel guides. . . . [My] responsibility is to update a fifth of the Germany guide for the 2007 edition. . . . In the fall, I will start working for MMG Partners. . . . This fall, I plan to apply to Judgment and Decision Making PhD programs, and hope to study behavior at the intersection of Economics and Psychology." I was happy to receive this update. By the fall of 2006, we had Lisa's doctoral application, and by the fall of 2007, she was back at Harvard, working with both Gilbert and me.

Francesca collaborated on most of the research I published with Lisa, which eventually included five empirical papers, including the 2012 and 2020 signing-first papers. Lisa received her doctorate from Harvard in 2012 and moved on to a two-year postdoc at Northwestern, followed by a tenure-track position at the London Business School in 2014. Lisa remained a close friend throughout this time, and I proudly officiated at her wedding on October 11, 2015, to Matt Wilson, as announced in the *New York Times*:

> Lisa Lixin Shu, the daughter of Jieqi Wu and Benjamin Shu of Bayside, N.Y., is to be married on Sunday to Matthew Julius Wilson, the son of Linda E. Sopp and Robert H. Wilson of Northampton, Mass. Max H. Bazerman, the bride's doctoral adviser, who became a Universal Life minister for the occasion, is to officiate at the Harvard Club of New York in Manhattan.[6]

Lisa eventually decided to leave academia in 2019 to get involved in a variety of organizations that help early-stage business founders acquire the negotiation skills they need to help them succeed. She remains a valued friend.

## Dan Ariely

Ariely is a very famous academic. He received two doctoral degrees, one in cognitive psychology from the University of North Carolina and a second in marketing from Duke University in 1998. That year, Ariely accepted a faculty position at MIT. His real-world fame spiked in 2008 with the publication of *Predictably Irrational*, a best-selling book on decision-making.

Prior to our collaboration on the signing-first paper, Ariely and I had occasional interactions. In 2005, while Ariely was at MIT and I was at HBS, we interacted about the possible cross-listing of courses between Harvard and MIT in the areas of social psychology, decision-making, and behavioral economics. Nothing developed from those communications.

In 2006, Ariely conducted experiments at MIT in which participants received electric shocks. The experiments lacked the required ethics committee approval.[7] After an internal review, MIT's ethics committee prohibited Ariely from conducting experiments. He left MIT and moved to Duke in 2008. In 2010, Ariely claimed in an NPR interview that data from the insurance company Delta Dental showed that dentists misdiagnosed cavities when analyzing X-rays more than half the time.[8] A spokesperson for Delta Dental contradicted this claim by noting that the company does not collect data that could even test such a claim.[9] I had a vague sense of the MIT episode when we combined efforts on the signing-first project but had not heard the Delta Dental story.

While my relationship with Ariely was minimal prior to the signing-first project, and consistently negative since I first questioned the insurance data, Gino had been a friend of Ariely from the time when they both lived in North Carolina. They published papers together, and Gino consistently spoke positively of Ariely and the kind things he had done for those around him.

By the time Ariely published his book *The (Honest) Truth About Dishonesty* in 2012, my interactions with him were limited, and our emails were more often contentious than not.[10] Nonetheless, he included me in his "list of collaborators" at the end of the book, writing:

> Max is insightful about pretty much any topic that comes up in research, politics, and personal life. And he always has something unexpected and interesting to say. After finding out that many of his students solve their own dilemmas by asking themselves, "What would Max do?," I tried this approach a few times

myself and can attest to its usefulness. Max is currently a professor at Harvard University.

I found this tribute to be odd, as we had connected very little, and our only collaborative work was the 2012 paper. I didn't know why he had decided to mention me in the book.

In the aftermath of the 2021 Data Colada post about the insurance study in our paper, a 2022 investigation by Hamakor, an Israeli television program, suggested that many of Ariely's studies were not reproducible. The show questioned the reliability of Ariely's work, including the signing-first study. The show raised questions about how Ariely carried out his studies, how he collected data, and whether he had carried out certain studies at all.

One example was his well-known "Ten Commandments" study with On Amir and Nina Mazar, which claims that prompting people to recall the Ten Commandments before taking a test reduces cheating.[11] Ariely claimed the data were collected at UCLA with assistance from Professor Aimee Drolet Rossi. However, Drolet Rossi denies she ran the study. I have only met Drolet Rossi a couple of times. Yet her vehemence against Ariely for involving her in his story led her to contact me in 2024, given my role in the signing-first story and her knowledge that I was writing about the alleged frauds. She couldn't have been clearer in stating she had had nothing to do with the collection of the data for the Ten Commandments study. After investigating, UCLA issued a formal statement supporting Drolet Rossi's account that the experiment did not take place at that university. In an interview with the *Chronicle of Higher Education*, Drolet Rossi called Ariely a "smart guy but a charlatan."[12]

A 2023 *New Yorker* article about the Gino and Ariely scandal cites a senior researcher, who asks of Ariely:

> How do you swim through that murky area of where is he lying? Where is he stretching the truth? What is he forgetting or misremembering? Because he does all three of those things very consistently. So when it really matters—like with the auto insurance—which of these three things is it?[13]

Nobel Prize–winning economist Richard Thaler tweeted after the 2021 Data Colada post that he had "known for years that Dan Ariely made stuff up."[14] And the *Chronicle of Higher Education* documents that behavioral economist George Loewenstein, whom Ariely has called "my role model,"[15] made clear that he's lost faith in Ariely's work: "I have no idea if the data are real. . . . I can't feel confident about anything where he collected and analyzed the data."[16]

## Nina Mazar

Mazar was born and raised in Germany to parents from Croatia and Serbia. She completed her doctorate at the Johannes-Gutenberg University in Mainz, Germany, and then became a postdoctoral associate of Ariely at MIT.[17] Her first faculty position was at the University of Toronto. Mazar, like Gino, was named one of the "Best 40 Under 40" B-school professors by Poets and Quants, in 2014. While at Toronto, Mazar, along with Ariely, was a cofounder and chief scientific adviser of BEworks, a consulting firm that focuses on applying behavioral science to commercial problems. She took an academic leave from Toronto to work at the World Bank's behavioral insights initiative, eMBeD, from 2015 to 2017. In 2018, Mazar took a faculty position at Boston University.[18]

During the 2011–2012 creation of the signing-first paper, Mazar seemed to be in charge of interacting with the author group on behalf of Ariely, though I didn't know this for certain. As described in chapter 1, I first met Mazar in person in January 2012, when Shu introduced us in the hallway of an academic conference and Mazar tried to explain the puzzling data in the insurance study. I found Mazar to be helpful at the time, as she seemed to resolve, with a delay, some of the problems I had had with Ariely. At the same time, she didn't seem to be troubled by Ariely's evasive, abrupt, and misleading communications regarding the study. While I find Mazar's trust in Ariely perplexing, one of my mentees pointed out to me that this can easily be explained by the fact that Ariely was Mazar's postdoctoral adviser and that she likely placed a great deal of trust in him (for better or worse). Shu and Mazar were also interacting directly with each other at the time and seemed to work together well. But once our expanded team began writing the 2020 replication-failure paper, I found Mazar consistently siding with Ariely's preference to discount the evidence that signing first didn't work.

In 2022, I wrote a chapter for my book *Complicit* describing the replication failure, the alleged fraud in Study 3, and my complicity in not noticing and acting on this alleged fraud sooner. I asked Shu, Mazar, Gino, and Ariely to review an early draft for any factually incorrect information. In that draft, I referred to the insurance study as the "Mazar and Ariely study." Mazar responded to this characterization with annoyance. She was no more involved in the insurance study than I had been, she wrote in an email, and she had only joined the project at the point when the three studies were put together. This surprised me, as Ariely had said that if he joined the combined project, Mazar would need to be included because of her being part of the insurance study. I was left confused about why Mazar was included in the combined project if she hadn't been involved in the insurance study. At the same time, I had little evidence to refute what Mazar told me in 2022. And, as I write this book, I believe that Mazar was not involved in the data collection of the insurance study but rather was pulled in by her mentor, Ariely, to serve as a connector between the two subprojects.

**Closing Comments**

By describing my relationships with my co-authors on the signing-first paper, I have aimed to convey the context in which the paper developed. As later chapters of this book will make clear, I could have intervened more strongly at many points in the development of our fraudulent paper. I am not shy, nor do I hide from conflict, yet I didn't do enough. I failed to do more in part because I relied on people with whom I had collaborative relationships—and trusted people who, in the end, may not have been trustworthy.

I trusted the ability and integrity of my co-authors on the 2012 paper, just as I have trusted many past co-authors. When I worked with relatively new doctoral students, I didn't always fully trust their ability to conduct research unsupervised because of their lack of experience. Even in these cases, though, I generally trusted a more senior doctoral student to oversee their work. If there was no senior doctoral student on the project, I may have carefully reviewed these students' work. However, I never questioned the integrity of data provided by a co-author. And, as noted earlier, there are many upsides to this type of trust.

This story of allowing unethical behavior to develop in part out of trust is far from unique. Most scandals reported in the media have included complicitors who allowed harm-doers to engage in destructive behavior over time. Often, the nature of the relationships between the parties involved explains this trust. In *Complicit*, I document this pattern across many crises, including the child abuse crimes covered up by Penn State, Michigan State, and the Catholic Church, as well as scandals at Theranos, WeWork, and Volkswagen.[19]

I built my career based on trusting people younger and smarter than me, people with more contemporary methodological skills. As a result, over time, I have moved farther and farther away from the raw data in my research. This type of diffusion of responsibility in social science research is common. While trust, strong relationships, and diffusing responsibility tend to be beneficial overall, going forward, I will be closer to my colleagues' data collection processes than I have been in the past. I still want to trust my co-authors, but I will verify their trustworthiness. Many think that being trusting is part of being an ethical person. I now argue that we need to go beyond this simple assumption and explore when it is our obligation to trust, but verify.

# 3 Crisis or Renaissance?

The data-fabrication story that I relate in this book is just one credibility crisis that the field of psychology has faced over time. Dating back to the birth of psychology as a science in the late nineteenth century, credibility has always been a challenge for the field and for social science more broadly. Pseudotherapies that predate psychological science were practiced by some wizards, sorcerers, charmers, shamans, medicine men, seers, and religious figures.[1] These since debunked pseudotherapies included phrenology (which claimed to offer insights into individuals by measuring aspects of their head), physiognomy (judging someone's character based on observations of their face), mesmerism (attempted healing with magnets), and spiritualism (which included a variety of invalid paranormal views).[2] Even the Harvard psychologist William James, perhaps the most important figure in the early development of psychology as a science, studied paranormal activities in ways that would seem nonsensical to the scientific community today.[3]

In 1909, Sigmund Freud made his first and only trip to America, giving five introductory lectures on psychoanalysis. Psychoanalysis had little use for the then emerging experimental or scientific approaches to the study of the mind, and what being a psychologist would mean to the public was up for grabs. Psychoanalysis found a home in academic institutions, but psychoanalytic approaches and psychological science rooted in the scientific method have been in conflict ever since. Despite extensive developments in psychological science over the past 150 years, the public has often lacked clarity on the distinctions among pseudotherapies, psychoanalysis, and other forms of talk therapy, and between those practices and knowledge gained from research carefully conducted by scholars with scientific credentials. Even today, saying you are a psychologist at a social event doesn't convey whether what you have to offer is based on valid science.

While these tensions were present at the start of the current century, psychological science had arrived. The status of psychology as a legitimate science was well established. University psychology departments grew significantly from 1990 to 2010, and their reputation improved.[4] Professional schools in universities, and particularly business schools, began hiring PhDs in psychology, organizational behavior, and other areas that included training in psychological science. Psychology was also influencing other disciplines, including the emerging field of behavioral economics and the related areas of behavioral finance, behavioral marketing, and so on. In 2002, Daniel Kahneman, a psychologist, won the Nobel Prize in Economics.

Many scholars with scientific training in psychology found that managers welcomed our teaching—in the form of lucrative executive education and consulting work. The broader intellectual public was interested as well. Kahneman's *Thinking, Fast and Slow*, Carol Dweck's *Mindset: The New Psychology of Success*, and Adam Grant's *Hidden Potential: The Science of Achieving Great Things* each sold more than a million copies.[5] Psychology was embraced on a wide variety of social media platforms, including TED Talks, podcasts, Twitter (X), and Facebook. The growing prevalence of citations of psychology journals in Wikipedia entries, depicted in figure 3.1, provides one indicator of the increased interest in psychology, and particularly social psychology, to the broader public. While the overall number of entries in Wikipedia certainly grew over the same period, the growth of citations in social psychology remains noteworthy.

In many ways, the first decade of the twenty-first century was a fine time to have expertise in psychological science. The popularization of psychology brought with it a shift in incentives for researchers. We found ourselves navigating a landscape where the impact of our work was measured not just by its scientific rigor and publication in prestigious journals but also by its resonance with the public. The credibility of psychological science, and of social psychology specifically, had improved. But challenges to psychology's credibility would soon reemerge.

**The Crisis Begins**

In 2011, the most prestigious journal in social psychology, the *Journal of Personality and Social Psychology*, published an article by the well-respected Cornell University psychologist Daryl Bem[6] that put forth "a transparently

# Crisis or Renaissance?

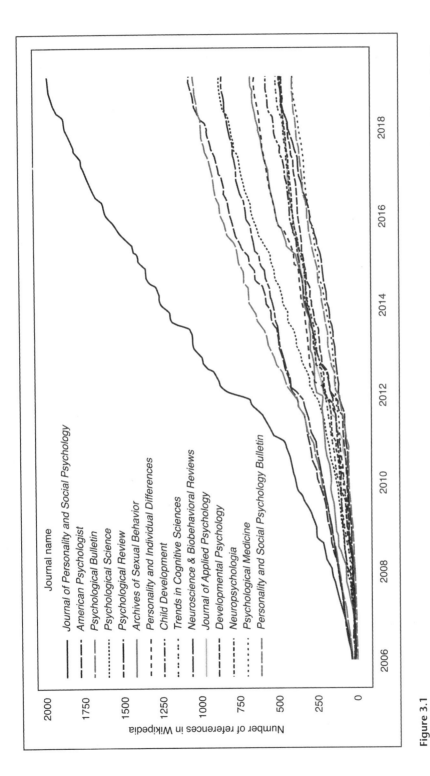

**Figure 3.1**

The number of citations to psychology journals in all Wikipedia articles. *Source*: N. Banasik-Jemielniak, D. Jemielniak, and M. Wilamowski, "Psychology and Wikipedia: Measuring Psychology Journals' Impact by Wikipedia Citations," *Social Science Computer Review* 40, no. 3 (2022): 756–774. https://doi.org/10.1177/08944393211993836.

outlandish claim—that people can be influenced by an unforeseeable future event," in the words of the Data Colada team.[7] In the paper, Bem claimed to have used scientific methods in nine experiments to support the existence of a type of extrasensory perception (ESP) known as precognition—the sense of knowing what will happen in the future. Reminiscent of William James's paranormal interests over one hundred years earlier, the publication by a prestigious psychology journal of work by a respected senior scholar in support of ESP was shocking. Many psychologists were embarrassed that their field would allow such invalid work to be published. I was stunned that the journal accepted this work.

In one of the experiments, participants were (1) given several minutes to examine a number of words, (2) then given additional time to type out a subset of those words, and (3) with the words taken away, asked to list as many of the words they had seen as possible.

Not surprisingly, they were much more likely to remember words they had encountered twice—those they had seen and then typed. In the experimental condition of interest, Bem flipped the second and third tasks, so that participants were asked to recall words before being asked to type a subset of those words. Bem claimed to have found evidence that these study participants were better at remembering the words they would later encounter a second time—based on ESP. All nine studies defied what is known about physical science, contradicting well-substantiated theories in both physics and biology.

The response from the social science community was one of disbelief. Researchers critiqued Bem's methods, the statistical tests he used, and his failure to report studies that did not support his beliefs in ESP. Multiple research groups went to the trouble of trying to replicate Bem's findings, consistently without success. In a 2011 paper published in the *Review of General Psychology*, psychologists Etienne LeBel of the University of Western Ontario and Kurt Peters of Norwich University used Bem's paper as a jumping-off point to discuss how experimental psychology is systemically biased to interpret data in ways that favor researchers' theories.[8] Also in 2011, in the same journal that published Bem's original experiments, the *Journal of Personality and Social Psychology*, psychologists Jeff Galak of Carnegie Mellon University, Robyn A. LeBoeuf of the University of Florida, Leif D. Nelson, and Joseph P. Simmons provided seven experiments testing for precognition that "found no evidence supporting its existence."[9] A further large-scale preregistered replication in 2023 found no evidence to support Bem.[10]

"I'm all for rigor, but I prefer other people do it," Bem told *Slate* magazine in 2017. "I see its importance—it's fun for some people—but I don't have the patience for it."[11] Bem continued, "If you looked at all my past experiments, they were always rhetorical devices. I gathered data to show how my point would be made. I used data as a point of persuasion, and I never really worried about, 'Will this replicate or will this not?'"[12] These are shocking statements from a well-respected scientist. The ridiculousness of Bem's research being published in a leading social psychology journal is often credited as prompting the revolution to improve the integrity of social science research.

**Data Colada and P-Hacking**

As you know by now, two of the co-authors on the 2012 paper that failed to replicate Bem's findings, Leif Nelson and Joseph Simmons, would go on to form the Data Colada trio with Uri Simonsohn. Nelson and Simmons had attended graduate school together at Princeton; they had played in a cover band together and belonged to the same softball team.[13] Nelson met Simonsohn in 2007 when they were faculty members at the University of California, San Diego. The three of them published an influential paper on p-hacking in 2011[14] and launched Data Colada in September 2013 as a blog focused on investigating research for replicability.[15]

The importance of Simmons, Nelson, and Simonsohn's 2011 p-hacking paper requires a bit of understanding of the scientific method and how social scientists use the concept of statistical significance. The scientific method developed as early as the seventeenth century.[16] The goal of the scientific method is to use a process that objectively tests a scientist's idea. A scientist develops an idea based on the existing literature and observations of the world. Using this information, the scientist formulates a hypothesis that specifies a concrete prediction that can be tested. The scientist then develops a method (e.g., an experiment) for collecting data, collects that data, and statistically tests the data to see whether the hypothesis is confirmed.

Statistical significance assesses the likelihood that experimental results can be explained solely by chance. A statistically significant result at the

.05 level means there is less than a one in twenty (5 percent) chance that the result would have been found absent the tested relationship being true. Most social scientists and journals have worked under a norm requiring results to be significant at the .05 level for publication. So, when a researcher finds that the height of basketball players is positively related to points scored per game, and the data are statistically significant at the .05 level, this means there is a less than 5 percent chance of finding this result from random data.

But what if the same researcher also tested the relationship between player height and number of points scored per minute played instead of points scored per game? Or what if they tested the relationship by categorizing players' height into three groups, short, medium, and tall? What if the researcher tested the predicted relationship in multiple different groups of players? Or what if the researcher tested the predicted relationship both before and after the NBA started awarding three points rather than two for shots taken beyond a certain distance from the basket? Notice that if you were to find the hypothesized relationship one in twenty times using random data when the effect does not actually exist, if you make multiple attempts to find a link between height and points scored, your likelihood of finding a significant effect at the .05 level in at least one of these tests will be much higher than if you had made only one attempt. Simmons, Nelson, and Simonsohn's 2011 p-hacking paper alerted the social science research community to the surprisingly large increase in the likelihood of confirming predictions that are not true by running tests in multiple ways and selectively reporting data and analyses, a practice they coined *p-hacking*.

Prior to the 2011 p-hacking paper, many researchers naïvely p-hacked without realizing they were violating the appropriate logic of statistical testing. Common violations included the following:

- Looking at the data as they were being collected and stopping experiments once the results supported the researcher's prediction and were statistically significant. A variation of this strategy would be to run an experiment with twenty study participants per condition, check for significance, and, if the results were significant, stop collecting data; if the data were in the right direction but fell short of significance, add another ten study participants per condition.

- Removing data points that were too extreme to be reasonable. Many researchers eliminated what they viewed as unreasonable data points.

The problem with this strategy was that even an honest researcher might have had a biased view of which data points should be viewed as outliers, thereby increasing the likelihood of finding a predicted effect.

- Categorizing observations in multiple different ways. Variables could be treated continuously (e.g., height in inches) or in categories (below or above 66 inches). If data were collected in two locations (e.g., in two universities where two different co-authors were on the faculty), should the researcher test location A, location B, or the combined group? Some researchers answered this question based on which test "worked"—which one produced the predicted result.
- Collecting multiple dependent variables (outcomes such as: Did the patient die? How many days did they spend in the hospital? Are they happy with their medical care?) and only reporting on the one that confirmed the researcher's prediction, or changing the dependent variable of interest after data collection started.

In their 2011 paper, Simmons, Nelson, and Simonsohn included a satirical demonstration of the power of p-hacking by "finding" the ridiculous result that listening to the Beatles' song "When I'm 64" makes people younger. They imply that their results show that listening to the song changes your objective age. How could they have "proved" such an obviously wrong conclusion? University of Pennsylvania undergraduates who listened to "When I'm 64" during the experiment happened to be younger than a group of participants who listened to a different song (which will happen one out of twenty times with random data). As a result, Simmons and colleagues were able to "show" that listening to "When I'm 64" was related to age, when in fact they were simply paying attention to the one effect that happened to occur based on random variation. The trio also collected data from a third test condition, in which study participants listened to the song "Hot Potato," but did not use that condition when the results turned out not to be significant. They also collected data on the study participants' mothers' ages, fathers' ages, whether they would go to an early-bird special at a restaurant, and many other age-related variables. This gave the researchers many chances to compare many different variables with different statistical tests so that they could torture the data into submission. When one of these tests randomly worked at the .05 level of significance, the researchers "concluded" that listening to the Beatles' song makes you younger.

Around the time the trio was working on the p-hacking, or false positives, paper, researchers Leslie John (my colleague at Harvard Business School), George Loewenstein (Carnegie Mellon University), and Drazen Prelec (MIT) were documenting the surprisingly high rates at which psychological researchers were admitting to engaging in questionable research practices—practices that allowed for what would soon be known as p-hacking.[17] They surveyed over two thousand research psychologists to find out how frequently they engaged in questionable research practices, such as choosing not to report all study findings, collecting more data when no results had been found initially, or straightforwardly falsifying data. Surprisingly, 64 percent of the respondents admitted to engaging in the practices once or twice, 26 percent occasionally, and about 10 percent frequently.

Also in 2012, psychologist Stéphane Doyen and his colleagues reported a failure to replicate a well-known psychology study on priming led by John Bargh, an eminent social psychologist at Yale.[18] Bargh was best known for work on the impact of unconscious processes on behavior. In a 1996 paper, Bargh and his two junior colleagues showed the surprising result that simply priming people to think about being old would lead them to walk more slowly, as measured by the experimenters with stopwatches. Specifically, the researchers asked study participants to work on a word task. Some of the participants were exposed to words related to aging, such as *Florida* and *Bingo*; others were not shown aging-related words. The task was meant to "prime" participants to think about aging. Bargh and colleagues reported that the participants who were exposed to words related to aging walked more slowly when they left the lab than did those who had not seen aging-related words.[19] This very highly cited paper was one of a flurry of social psychology papers published on the influential effects of priming. Priming studies received significant media attention based on their surprising results but were met with skepticism by many researchers, who found the reported effects too large for the impact that such a subtle manipulation would be expected to have.

In two experiments, Doyen and his team were unable to replicate Bargh and colleagues' study. In one of the experiments, Doyen and colleagues used an automated electronic system to measure how quickly participants walked (a more precise measure than a stopwatch) and a larger sample than Bargh, and they didn't find the effect: Participants exposed to the prime didn't walk slower when they left the room. This led the research team to suspect that Bargh's experimenter(s) might have cued participants to slow down when leaving the room—for instance, by speaking or moving more slowly.[20] In a second experiment, Doyen and colleagues led half of those running the experiment to believe that participants would walk slower after being primed and led the other half of the experimenters to expect the participants would instead walk faster. The results showed that participants were clocked as walking slower only when the experimenters were led to believe they would do so. This suggests it was experimenter expectations that drove the priming effect, not the subconscious processes of the study participants.[21]

Bargh responded to the failure-to-replicate paper with a blog post that was covered in the media.[22] His response dealt in part with the substance of the experiment; for example, he insisted that the experimenter in his study had no knowledge of the study hypotheses, a claim that others disputed. Bargh's responses also included unnecessary insults: He called Doyen's team "incompetent or ill-informed" and implied that the journal that published their article had low standards.[23]

Bargh's defensive response drew the attention of psychologist and Nobel laureate Daniel Kahneman, who on September 26, 2012, wrote an email to priming researchers that expressed concern about credibility problems in their field, including replication failures, methodological problems, and outright fraud. Kahneman, who noted that he was "not a member of your community" but rather a "general believer" in priming who had written about priming research, wrote:

> For all these reasons, your field is now the poster child for doubts about the integrity of psychological research. Your problem is not with the few people who have actively challenged the validity of some priming results. It is with the much larger population of colleagues who in the past accepted your surprising results as facts when they were published. These people have now attached a question mark to the field, and it is your responsibility to remove it.[24]

Kahneman encouraged priming researchers to "collectively do something about this mess," which he warned could follow two other discredited areas of psychology research, subliminal perception and dissonance reduction, into a "profound eclipse." He encouraged the priming research community to face their critics' doubts directly by conducting credible replication studies.

The general view toward priming research became more skeptical, with many pointing to p-hacking as a likely culprit in the replication failures.

But Norbert Schwarz, a social psychologist who received Kahneman's email, responded by arguing that priming studies received skeptical attention because of their nonintuitive results, not because of p-hacking. "There is no empirical evidence that work in this area is more or less replicable than work in other areas," he told *Nature*.[25] In the years that followed Kahneman's missive, few replications of priming were published, and the credibility of priming research continued to decline.

In 2010, psychologists Dana Carney (UC Berkeley), Amy Cuddy (then my colleague at HBS), and Andy Yap (INSEAD) published a paper that claimed to show that posing in a position of dominance and power (e.g., with arms on hips and legs anchored in a wide stance) for as little as two minutes, a practice they dubbed "power posing," increased people's feelings of power, tolerance for risk, and testosterone levels, and decreased their cortisol (stress) levels.[26] The study included only forty-two participants in one experiment. Both having so few participants and conducting only one experiment were unusual at the time of this publication. In 2012, Cuddy gave a TED Talk that encouraged people to improve their lives by power posing. It went on to become one of the most popular TED Talks: As of 2025, it had been viewed over 70 million times.[27]

The media and public loved the idea of power posing, which offered an easy hack for doing well in interviews and other high-stress situations where one might want to feel more powerful. The TED Talk paved the way for Cuddy's best-selling book, *Presence: Bringing Your Boldest Self to Your Biggest Challenges*.[28] Power posing became one of the most well-known psychological effects. Over time, however, social scientists were less impressed by power posing. Many efforts failed to replicate the effect, and p-hacking was suspected. In 2015, for example, Eva Ranehill and colleagues published a paper that failed to replicate the original power-posing study with a much larger sample size.[29]

Carney, Cuddy, and Yap responded to these criticisms by publishing a 2015 paper that overviewed thirty-three somewhat related studies that appeared to support the claims of their paper.[30] Joe Simmons and Uri Simonsohn soon posted a response on Data Colada that suggested the studies included in the review were severely p-hacked.[31] By 2016, lead author Dana Carney had disavowed power posing on her Berkeley faculty web page: "As evidence has come in over these past 2+ years, my views have updated to reflect the evidence. <u>As such, I do not believe that 'power pose' effects</u>

are real."³² Amid the controversy, Cuddy voluntarily left her tenure-track position at HBS in the spring of 2017. But she continues to promote power posing to improve one's life, has defended her work on the topic, and has published evidence tangential to the claims of the original power-posing paper.³³ The popularity of power posing and its failure to replicate made it the most commonly cited example of the replicability crisis in psychology.

**Fraud versus P-Hacking**

Around the same time that p-hacking was emerging as a threat to the credibility of psychological research, data fabrications, or outright frauds, were also being discovered. Across agencies, U.S. federal policy includes both fabrication and falsification as fraudulent research activities. Fabrication involves making up data or results.³⁴ Falsification is defined as the intentional manipulation of research materials, equipment, or processes, or changing or omitting data or results, such that the research is not accurately represented in the reporting of the research. Chapter 8 details the major scientific frauds in psychology during this time; they included revelations about Marc Hauser of Harvard in 2010, Diederik Stapel of Tilburg University in 2011, Dirk Smeesters of Erasmus University in 2011, and Lawrence Sanna of the University of Michigan in 2012. All resigned and left academia. Uri Simonsohn discovered the fraud of both Smeesters and Sanna.

Both p-hacking and fraud led to the publication of results that would later fail to replicate. Yet during this time, these two replicability challenges differed in important respects. P-hacking tended to qualify as implicit unethical behavior; that is, the researcher or researchers were not consciously aware they were doing something wrong. In contrast, fraudsters were aware of their ethical violations. P-hackers tended to massage their data sufficiently to get a result over the hurdle of significance. Data Colada ultimately concluded that when a researcher generates many experimental results that are just barely significant, this is a sign of p-hacking. In contrast, fraudulent results are often bold, larger effects.³⁵

In the past fifteen years, social science has changed its attitude toward p-hackers. As the reform movement started, Data Colada and others were quick to note that most p-hacking was unintentional, most social scientists were guilty of it to some degree, and it was simply time for reform, not punishment. On a personal level, independent of explicitly recognizing the statistical harms of obtaining too many tests of the same idea, my research typically followed a more statistically justifiable pattern that avoided p-hacking. For example, I was never an enthusiast for collecting multiple dependent variables or for post hoc explorations of data. But I would not be shocked if some co-author had a memory of my authorization to use my funding to collect additional study participants. The Data Colada trio even admitted to p-hacking in the past, before their 2011 paper clarified the harm created by the practice. Today, social scientists are expected to be aware of the problems of p-hacking, and p-hackers are typically guilty of more intentional violations.

### The Magnitude of the Replicability Crisis

In 2012, University of Virginia psychology professor Brian Nosek co-founded the Center for Open Science (COS) with Jeffrey Spies. The COS is a nonprofit platform whose mission is to "increase the openness, integrity, and reproducibility of scientific research by assisting researchers, journals, funders, and universities to develop policies that will create more reproducible research"—that is, research with less fraud and less p-hacking. COS, now generally viewed as the center of what is called the open science movement, offers tools to encourage scientists to use best scientific practices, share data, and conduct their work more transparently.

One of COS's most important efforts was a large-scale initiative, led by Nosek, to replicate one hundred studies published in three of the most prestigious psychology journals—*Psychological Science*, the *Journal of Personality and Social Psychology*, and the *Journal of Experimental Psychology: Learning, Memory, and Cognition*—to see if the results could be replicated.[36] *Science* reported the results of the effort in 2015. While ninety-seven of the original studies reported significant effects at the .05 level, only 36 percent of the replications were significant.[37]

The well-known social scientists Dan Gilbert, Gary King, Stephen Pettigrew, and Tim Wilson published an article, also in *Science*, that was very critical of aspects of the Nosek-led publication.[38] Gilbert and colleagues argued that the Nosek team had failed to consider the expected failures in social science research, that they had focused on weaker studies with small samples, that the replication studies differed too much from the original studies, that the selection process for identifying studies wasn't blind, and that the Nosek team was biased toward finding replication failures. Gilbert's team also mocked the experimenters who ran the replications as incompetent and concluded that "the reproducibility of psychological science is quite high."[39]

While Gilbert and colleagues made some relevant methodological critiques, most social scientists, including me, remained stunned by the magnitude of the replication failures documented by the Nosek team. Yet many social psychologists were upset, believing that the media headline that over half of the studies could not be replicated provided an exaggerated view of the problem. Some social psychologists were also upset that the debate played out in public and discredited the field, rather than occurring internally.

Combined with Data Colada's efforts, the Nosek-led project firmly highlighted what has been called a replication crisis—the belief that too many published results in the social sciences cannot be replicated. Many maintain that the replication crisis in social science arose somewhere between Data Colada's 2011 paper and the Nosek team's 2015 publication. But the Data Colada team published a review paper in 2018 arguing against this term, as they noted that problems of replication had long existed. Making the problems in psychology transparent allowed the field to be reborn, they argued, and they positioned the open science movement as "psychology's renaissance."[40]

The response to the crisis within the research community varied. Some became enthusiastic supporters of the open science movement, changed how they conducted research, and contributed to efforts to reform social science (which I detail in chapter 12). Daniel Kahneman described Data Colada to the *New Yorker* as "heroes of mine" and said he regretted his previous support of research findings that the blog later showed were faulty. Many researchers gradually adjusted their research practices as journals started to require changes. Yet others found the crisis to be overstated and destructive to psychology. Schwarz called the reform movement a "witch hunt,"[41] and Gilbert described the so-called "replication police" as "shameless little bullies."[42]

Data Colada has also been accused of sexism. In a $25 million lawsuit against the Data Colada trio and HBS, Gino alleged she had been treated unfairly owing in part to gender discrimination. Citing Data Colada's criticisms of Amy Cuddy's research on power posing, Gino said in her lawsuit that the team "targeted the work of prominent female academics and subjected it to an exceptionally high level of public scrutiny."[43] Others have also described the treatment of Amy Cuddy as sexist. "Data Colada's harshest critics saw the young men as jealous upstarts who didn't understand the soft artistry of the social sciences," the *New Yorker* reported.[44] In contrast, Simine Vazire, an important data reformer whom you will meet later in this chapter, argued in a tweet, "Powerful people using sexism as a shield :( I'm sure Gino & Cuddy are targets of sexism & worse. But scholarly criticism of their work, eg Data Colada's, isn't sexism. Saying it is undermines efforts to combat actual sexism & erodes our field's credibility by silencing criticism."[45] In my view, the Data Colada trio can be blunt and tough, and may often skip social pleasantries. And, while I have heard many claims about the possibility of members of Data Colada being sexist both before and after the Gino story, I see little evidence that sexism played a central role in their posts about Cuddy or Gino.

Others have criticized the Data Colada trio for self-appointing themselves the authorities in charge of adjudicating data fraud. Data Colada should be working instead to institutionalize an auditing function within more established organizations, these critics argue. I certainly know of multiple scholars with high integrity who felt intimated by Data Colada. Scholars have reported being investigated by Data Colada, without justification from their perspective. The trio have also been accused of conducting nonrandom audits. Some wonder whether they would attack a close friend—although, it should be noted, Ariely was Simonsohn's postdoc adviser. Others object to the wry sense of humor that crops up in Data Colada posts as they argue very serious matters.

Another argument from those resisting change has been based on the myth of the self-correcting nature of science.[46] This argument suggests that false findings will eventually be discovered and rooted out, leaving science in fine shape. The counterargument is that self-correction does not always occur, and the discovery and revelation of false results can be a very slow process. During this time, other researchers waste time and resources conducting experiments based on false results, and the wrong researchers are hired and promoted, creating injustice in what we represent to be a meritocratic system.

Barbara Spellman, editor of *Perspectives on Psychological Science* and a professor of psychology at the University of Virginia, has referred to the events between 2011 and 2015 as a "revolution."[47] Business schools paid attention to the crisis or revolution with a few years' delay compared to psychology departments. Spellman aptly described the conflicts in psychology as a battle between the older Generation 1.0 (both Spellman and I would fall into this generation), members of which developed their careers with p-hacking going unnoticed and few checks on replicability, and the younger Generation 2.0, which was actively pushing for change.[48] Similarly, Leif Nelson has described visiting other universities and finding a younger generation that treats Data Colada's arguments and evidence as obvious, while the older generation remains in denial and is sometimes confrontational.[49]

**Recognition of the Crisis**

One organizational response to the replication crisis was the 2016 founding of the Society for the Improvement of Psychological Science (SIPS) by Nosek and Simine Vazire. At the time, Vazire was a psychologist on the faculty of the University of California, Davis, and a known activist in the open science movement. SIPS was interested in bringing together psychologists who aimed to improve the integrity of psychological science. SIPS held its inaugural meeting in June 2016 in Charlottesville, Virginia, home to COS, and became connected to *Collabra: Psychology*, an open access journal taking active steps to improve the conduct of open science. By 2020, Vazire had become the journal's editor in chief.

Until very recently, the open science movement remained on the fringes of academic psychology. Some journals were changing their guidelines to promote more open science, but many did not. Signs of a broader shift in the field toward open science came in 2023, when *Psychological Science*, perhaps the most visible psychology research journal, announced that Vazire, by then a professor at the University of Melbourne, would become its new editor on January 1, 2024. Upon taking up the post at *Psychological Science*, Vazire announced the appointment of a new group of editors tasked with confirming that published articles were conducted in accordance with many of the recommendations core to the open science movement, including recommendations concerning statistics, transparency, and rigor.[50] Many of us in the field viewed Vazire's appointment as recognition by the mainstream psychological science community that it was time for change.

The scandal that is the focus of this book unfolded at the same time as the development of the open science movement that I've just described. This context will become important as I present how the story of Gino's alleged data fabrication unfolded and how various actors responded to it. We will also examine how the story could fuel future efforts to create a more reproducible world of social science. I return to the changes needed in the field in the last chapter of the book.

# 4 The Diffusion of Signing First

At the same time that the social science reform movement described in chapter 3 was developing, the 2012 signing-first paper was receiving a great deal of attention. The paper was very highly cited by other social scientists, generating over five hundred citations in other research papers by 2023.[1] Many organizations heard about the idea, liked it, and moved the signature line from the bottom of their forms to the top. I personally presented our work to corporations and to academic audiences. I was enthusiastic about the improved honesty that I believed organizations could achieve with a simple cut and paste of a signature line.

I was not alone. The 2015 *Social and Behavioral Sciences Team Annual Report* from the U.S. National Science and Technology Council, which advises the U.S. president, reported:

> To improve the accuracy of sales figures self-reported by vendors selling goods and services to the Government, SBST and the General Services Administration (GSA) redesigned an online data-entry form to include a signature box at the top of the page in which the user had to confirm the accuracy of self-reported sales. Because vendors pay to the Government a small fee based on those sales reports, introducing this box led to an additional $1.59 million in fees collected within a single quarter. Based on this result, GSA is making permanent changes to the form to incorporate a signature box."[2]

This study was never published, and the office failed to provide additional details about its evidence. The group that produced this report was the original "nudge" unit within the U.S. government.

In their 2008 book *Nudge*, behavioral economist Richard Thaler and legal scholar Cass Sunstein introduced the concept of nudges as a mechanism to influence hundreds, thousands, and even millions of people to make better or more ethical decisions.[3] *Nudge* offered a blueprint to help many of us in behavioral science find tweaks that could significantly improve the behaviors of many. Moving a signature line, requiring employees to opt out of their 401(k) rather than to opt in, and placing dessert less prominently in a cafeteria line are all simple examples of nudges.

By 2010 the Behavioural Insights Team (BIT), then a part of the UK's government, was the center of the applied world of nudges. As Michael Luca and I wrote in our book, *The Power of Experiments*, the members of the BIT team, led by David Halpern, "were skilled practitioners in using social science, combined with the logic of Thaler and Sunstein's choice architecture, to create an organization that would work to make governments more effective and provide a model for other organizations and governments to follow."[4] During my many discussions with BIT, I often advocated for the signing-first intervention, as I believed it worked and would be easy for governments to implement.

As I mentioned in chapter 2, in 2013, I had co-founded and co-led the Behavioral Insights Group at Harvard, which connected the many scholars at the university who ran social science field experiments. For a field course titled "UK: Behavioral Insights" that Michael Luca and I co-taught multiple times, we took more than thirty Harvard graduate students to London to work on a variety of field interventions with BIT's existing clients. I led efforts with BIT economist Michael Sanders (now at King's College) to apply for a $1 million grant from the Sloan Foundation, which we received, to coordinate the growing global behavioral science community.

BIT scientists ran hundreds of field experiments—sometimes with university-based academics, sometimes on their own, sometimes with members of organizations outside academia. In a 2014 talk, I presented to the BIT unit what I believed to be valid effects of signing first. Lisa Shu, then on the faculty of the London Business School, also presented this idea to the BIT unit. Years later, in an interview with NPR, Sanders recalled his reaction to the idea: "I exchanged glances with a couple of senior colleagues, and I said, we could do this in this area. We could do this in this area. There are so many opportunities for this."[5] Rather than assuming an effect from the literature would generalize to their real-world clients, the BIT unit's approach was to test ideas before rolling them out. So BIT ran multiple signing-first studies in the UK. None of them showed an effect for signing first. There are many reasons experiments might not show a predicted effect aside from the effect not being replicable, including weak execution. Unpublished studies typically lack sufficient information to assess why a null result occurred. The BIT's UK signing-first studies were not published, and I didn't know whether they had been well executed.

In 2017, Sanders and four co-authors published a paper on tax compliance in Guatemala.[6] This study tested multiple interventions to get people to pay their taxes, including having them sign a declaration that they would fill out the form honestly. The researchers found no increase in compliance for those who signed the declaration before filling out the form. However, the researchers noted multiple reasons why their intervention might have been weaker than the results published in our 2012 paper. Although I had trust in this research group, their failure to find an effect for signing first didn't much shake my enthusiasm for the idea.

Meanwhile, many organizations were moving the signature line from the bottom of forms to the top. It was particularly common for new forms and new online platforms to implement this idea since implementation online was simple. To take one example, Lemonade, an online insurance company that hired Ariely in 2016 as its chief behavioral officer, required customers to "sign their name to a digital pledge of honesty at the start of the claims process, rather than at the end," as *Fast Company* reported in 2017.[7]

## Cousin Stu

The insurance world also found me in 2016. Stuart Baserman, the co-founder of Slice Labs, a technology company that was helping the insurance industry move online, emailed me in September 2016. Without Stu's email, which he says he almost did not send, the fraud in our paper might not have been revealed. "A couple of days ago I was researching the 'psychology of claims' and I came across 'Signing at the beginning makes ethics salient,'" Stu wrote to me. "Of course, the paper and your name caught my attention. If you have some time, it would be nice to learn about you, your work and how it may relate to what we are building at Slice."

Stu and I connected by phone and exchanged many emails. In October 2016, he and his spouse, Sue, who live in Ottawa, Ontario, visited my spouse, Marla, and me at our vacation home in Stowe, Vermont. We became good friends, and that friendship has continued. And if you're wondering about our last names, so were we: My spouse ordered DNA-testing kits for Stu and for me, which showed that we are very distant cousins.

In late January 2017, Slice hired me to help induce honesty from online insurance claimants and to advise on a variety of high-level negotiations and strategic decisions facing the company. As part of my assignment to induce claimants to tell the truth online, I recommended having them sign a statement before filling out a claim form in which they promised to fill out the form truthfully. We frequently discussed testing the effectiveness of signing first online, but Slice had too few claimants to create a valid experiment. So they moved forward with having claimants sign first, in addition to adopting a number of other ideas from behavioral science for inducing honesty.

I really liked working with Stu, Slice CEO and co-founder Tim Attia, and others at Slice, and I believe they liked working with me. While working for Slice, I became fascinated with the uniqueness of the online context for inducing honesty and imagined that ideas for inducing online honesty could be applied beyond insurance claims to dating, reimbursement requests, tax collection, and other online contexts. Some aspects of inducing honesty online seemed more complicated than inducing honesty in telephone calls and on pen-and-paper forms, but other aspects of an online platform appeared to make it easier to prompt truthfulness. For example, when it came to the signing-first intervention, online claim forms could easily be programmed to not advance until the claimant attests to their honesty; by comparison, with pen and paper, claimants could fill out the form first and then return to the top of the form to sign. With my HBS colleague Amit Goldenberg, I documented the Slice story in an HBS teaching case.[8]

### The Basic Challenge of Inducing Honesty Online

By 2017, most of the empirical studies I was working on were related to ethics, and increasingly on how to induce more ethical behavior. As a result of my consulting work with Slice, I recognized the growing importance of adapting studies about honesty to the online environment.

By the summer of 2017, I was in discussions with Ariella Kristal (then a Harvard PhD student, now at Columbia) and Ashley Whillans (my HBS colleague) about research that would examine this broader question of online honesty. Because I knew Slice was interested in the results we might find, I reached out to HBS officials before we started collecting data to confirm that it would be OK for me to conduct the basic research using HBS resources, given the possible conflict of interest between the basic research and my work for a consulting client. HBS officials approved the research project, understanding that the work would be scholarly research intended for academic publication rather than consulting work.

Kristal, Whillans, and I brainstormed about a number of possible ways to induce honesty online, including the use of videos (Would people be less likely to exaggerate a claim if they had to film themselves making the claim?), reciprocity (Would people be less likely to exaggerate a claim if their insurance company had already made a commitment to them to be fair?), and so on. But, given the apparent enormous strengths of signing first, as suggested in the 2012 paper, signing first was the obvious place to begin. In the two laboratory studies reported in the 2012 paper, participants visited the lab in person, and data were collected using pen-and-paper means. Kristal, Whillans, and I expected our first online study would be a simple and successful extension of the 2012 results in an online context.

But that wasn't the case. Our first attempt at replication failed. The degree to which participants cheated in an online experimental task that paralleled Study 1 from the 2012 paper was not statistically affected by whether they signed before or after filling out an online form. Since at that time I fully believed the results of the 2012 paper, I argued that there was probably a quirk in how we implemented this first online study that affected the results. We made a number of small adjustments and again ran the experiment online. Once again, no difference turned up between signing before or after. Though I was still fairly confident in the concept of signing first, I was beginning to feel a bit hesitant. As the third, fourth, fifth, and sixth studies failed, including two with pen and paper, my confidence in signing first was shaken. Kristal, Whillans, and I now had six (four online, two written) failures to replicate what my co-authors of the 2012 paper and I had reported as a very large, statistically significant effect.

Kristal, Whillans, and I didn't know whether the effect simply wouldn't replicate or whether there was an important difference that we weren't seeing between the methods in the 2012 paper and our replication failures. Still, with each additional failure, all three of us were losing confidence in the signing-first effect. In the process, the project was shifting from finding a way to induce online honesty to reporting the repeated failure to replicate a well-known effect in the literature. Kristal, Whillans, and I agreed that the next step should be to conduct a pure replication of one of the laboratory studies from the 2012 paper but with a much larger sample of participants so that the results of the new study would be more valid.

Kristal and Whillans proposed that we invite the other four authors from the original paper (Shu, Mazar, Gino, and Ariely) to join the project to make the reconciliation between the 2012 project and the replication (failure) project more cooperative, rather than a confrontation between two camps. Given my past difficult interactions on that project, I had misgivings, but I wanted to support the cooperative spirit of my more junior colleagues, and I agreed. Shu, Mazar, Gino, and Ariely all agreed to join the effort. We worked relatively well together through the collection of data in the seventh experiment of the series started by Kristal, Whillans, and me. This seventh experiment included 1,235 participants (compared to 101 and 60 participants reported in the two laboratory experiments in the 2012 paper). Once again, we failed to replicate the signing-first effect: Participants' responses were not statistically different based on whether they signed before or after reporting.

**Conflicts Among the Original Authors**

By July 2019, it was time to write up the seven-experiment failure-to-replicate paper for publication. In the process of writing this paper, Kristal looked at the data from the 2012 paper. In the field experiment data, she found an unexplainable, huge difference between conditions in the *first* baseline odometer readings—the readings reported *before* customers were randomly assigned to signing before or after. Specifically, the baseline reported mileage for drivers signing *after* was 75,035 miles, while the baseline reported mileage for drivers signing *first* was 59,693. Social scientists would call this a "randomization failure" since you would expect very little difference between two groups if people have been randomly assigned to them and no intervention has yet taken place. Simple statistics show that the likelihood of the two conditions differing by this large amount by chance was less than 1 in 10,000. This raised the question of whether a randomized experiment had taken place. I expressed my concerns to all six co-authors on the new paper. Mazar and Ariely claimed that we had discussed this issue collectively in 2012. I have no memory of such a conversation, and in thoroughly searching my email records, I find no evidence of such a conversation. I am confident that I would not have agreed to include the study had I known about this difference in the before measure. Ariely also provided no explanation for the strange data, nor did he provide evidence of the conversation that he claimed took place. Yet 2012 is a long time ago, memories are fallible, and I have remained open to Ariely providing the evidence that this specific conversation took place in some form. We all agreed to document the enormous pre-measure difference in our 2020 publication.

This was not the only issue to confront. Kristal, Whillans, and I also disagreed with Mazar and Ariely on whether the new studies invalidated the results we published in 2012. Kristal, Whillans, and I believed that the signing-first effect did not replicate, while Mazar and Ariely preferred to limit the conclusions drawn in the failure-to-replicate paper. For example, in a July 8 email, Ariely wrote:

> Overall I think that the most ethical interpretation is with a baysian [sic] approach and to say that we had some belief in the effect before and now we belive [sic] in it less, but we should not claim that we have zero belief in it. It is certainly not the case that the second time to do a study should always count more than the first one (just imagine if this paper came before—would we have said that we now fully belive [sic] in the sign first? OF course not).

From my perspective, Ariely was choosing to ignore the massiveness of the replication failure, particularly the fact that the last study was powered by many more participants. From a Bayesian approach, or properly updating beliefs as new evidence is added, there was little basis to believe in the signing-first effect.

The seven of us documented our seven failures to replicate in the *Proceedings of the National Academy of Sciences (PNAS)*, the same journal that published our 2012 paper.[9] "The current paper updates the scientific record by showing that signing at the beginning is unlikely to be a simple solution for increasing honest reporting," we wrote. This wording reflected a compromise between opposing groups; I would have preferred a much stronger disavowal of signing first.

Although most of our research team's discussion in 2020 focused on problems with Study 3 (the insurance study), it disturbed me that our replication attempts had been modeled on Studies 1 and 2 of the 2012 paper. How did we run two successful laboratory studies in 2012, followed by seven failures to replicate in the 2020 paper? In the 2019–2020 period, Gino claimed that her lab manager at the University of North Carolina (where Gino had worked prior to Harvard) conducted the experiments, and she said she trusted the lab manager. She offered no further explanation for the 2012 laboratory studies not being reproducible. Despite my skepticism regarding the 2012 paper results, I still did not suspect blatant data fabrication in any of the studies. Moreover, the possibility of two seemingly independent data fabrications occurring in the same paper—a paper with my name on it—was not even on my radar screen.

Soon after the 2020 paper was published, the deputy executive editor of *PNAS* contacted Mazar, the corresponding author, to ask whether our original paper should be retracted (Mazar quickly forwarded the email to rest of the 2012 authors):

Hi Dr. Mazar,

I am contacting you as the corresponding author for your 2012 PNAS publication. We recently received the below question from a reader about your most recent PNAS article titled, "Signing at the beginning versus at the end does not decrease dishonesty." A reader asked:

*Hi PNAS,*

*I'm in the process of preparing a review paper, and I need to consider a PNAS article for inclusion in it.*

*Will you be retracting this article (*https://www.pnas.org/content/109/38/15197*) with the publication of this more recent article (*https://www.pnas.org/content/117/13/7103*)? In the latter, the original authors refuted the results published in their earlier paper.*

Retractions should be considered if the original study is flawed in a significant manner such that there is clear evidence that the findings are unreliable, either as a result of major error through miscalculation or experimental error. This is an unusual situation and we would appreciate your thoughts on the matter.

Sincerely,

Daniel Salsbury

In multiple emails with my co-authors, I continued to argue for retracting the paper. On July 27, 2020, Gino emailed me and the other authors of the 2012 paper, saying, "I don't think the new paper makes sense without the first one, and I think it'd be bad for the advancement of science to retract the first one at this point. . . . I am not sure why we would retract the paper now instead of having that done earlier without a second paper."

In an email sent the next day, Ariely also argued against retraction:

I am not aware of any experimental error—my guess is that it is just one of these times when the lab produces a different result for some reason—I am not suggesting any mistake. . . . I believe that over time the weight of the evidence will be in favor of the first result. . . . But, with the British data, that when we were writing the paper was not ready yet to be published—I believe that over time the weight of the evidence will be in favor of the first result. . . . But—we will see. This is the beautify [sic] of this process.

A few hours later, Ariely added, "I suspect that we will end up retracting the second paper. . . . My strong preference is to keep both papers out and let the science process do its job."

If you were confused by Ariely's reference to "the British data," you are not alone. I had no idea what British data he might have been referring to. When I eventually received a write-up of the study he was referring to, I found it had little to do with the difference between signing first versus signing after.

In the early stages of the signing-first story, I see Mazar's support of the data collected by Ariely as an act of trust in a valued colleague, just as I was guilty of regarding the data collection led by Gino. Thus I am sympathetic to how relationships may have affected her support of the insurance study. But as the mountain of evidence grew against the signing-first paper, Mazar continued her support of the original paper and clarified her opposition to retraction in an email:

> I do not see reason for retracting our paper given PNAS' criteria. As far as I know we do not have evidence that the findings of our three experiments are unreliable, either as a result of major error through miscalculation or experimental error. . . . From the email thread so far, it looks like the majority agrees that there is no need for retraction. Shall we respond to PNAS with that or is there more need for discussion?

"It is obvious to me that the original paper was based on unscientific and unethical reporting of data," I responded. "This is the basis of my preference to retract. I think we should all be embarrassed that our names are on the paper—I certainly am embarrassed by having my name on that paper. . . . I may be outvoted, but do not read me as being part of a consensus, Max." Mazar asked that I clarify what was unscientific and unethical about our original data reporting. "Reporting a randomized experiment where there was no randomization," I answered, referring to Study 3. "Lack of transparency about this issue. . . . Obfuscation to multiple questions that I asked in the creation of the original paper. . . . Not informing me of the lack of randomization during the creation of the paper."

Some co-authors may have believed that it was more helpful to the scientific record to keep both papers in print so that readers could continue to see the full range of evidence on the signing-first idea. It is useful to remember that, despite my harsh response, which upset many of my co-authors, the possibility of data fabrication in any of the studies still had not occurred to me. After this debate, conducted primarily through email, Shu and I were explicitly in favor of retracting the 2012 paper, while the majority, Gino, Mazar, and Ariely, were against retraction. Mazar sent an email to Salsbury, the *PNAS* editor, arguing against retraction and correctly stating that this was the majority view. I insisted on adding the following to the email that Mazar sent to Salsbury: "The majority consist of Nina Mazar, Francesca Gino, and Dan Ariely. Lisa Shu and Max Bazerman believe that the issues of the paper warrant retraction." The paper was not retracted in 2020.

### Reflections on the Conflicting Views of 2020

As I review this story from the point when Kristal, Whillans, and I invited the other four authors of the 2012 paper to join our failure-to-replicate project to Ariely, Gino, and Mazar's refusal to retract the paper in 2020, I conclude that I was clearly the most critical of the five 2012 co-authors and the most vocal in favor of retraction. Yet I wasn't vocal enough. I should have held my ground and, if others didn't join me, I should have emailed the journal directly and provided the editor with reasons for retraction.[10]

As I try to justify my willingness to compromise, I remember how overwhelmed many of us were in 2020 as we dealt with the complexities of the COVID-19 pandemic. By then, Gino was the unit head of my department at HBS, and she was not happy with many of my criticisms of her management; we clashed on many issues unrelated to the signing-first project. I was also concerned about Kristal (then a doctoral student in NOM) and Whillans (then an assistant professor in NOM) getting caught in the middle of the dispute. These are my excuses for not pushing harder to publicly reveal why I thought the paper should be retracted. In retrospect, I wish I had looked past all of these factors and been open about what I believed.

# 5 The Crisis

While attending graduate school at the ESSEC business school in Paris, Zoé Ziani worked on a dissertation that examined the instrumentality of networking behaviors—that is, what we gain and lose from professional networking in a strategic manner.[1] During her studies on the topic, Ziani read a paper that Tiziana Casciaro (University of Toronto), Gino, and Maryam Kouchaki (Northwestern University) had published in 2014 in the journal *Administrative Science Quarterly*. Gino and her colleagues concluded from their data that people who have a promotion mindset (i.e., a focus on achievement and accomplishment) tend to think about what they *want* to do, while those with a prevention mindset (focused on avoiding harm and minimizing losses) tend to think about what they *should* do; as a result, those with a promotion mindset are more comfortable engaging in self-promotion than those with a prevention mindset.

Study 3a of that paper, a lab experiment with data collection led by Gino, focused on the mindset of people engaged in networking. In the study, participants who were asked to think about a time when they networked in instrumental ways to promote themselves were more likely to complete words like "sh_ _er," "w _ _ h," and "s _ _ p" with words related to cleaning—shower, wash, and soap—than were study participants who simply thought about a time in which they networked (without necessarily having instrumental intentions). The research team predicted that study participants who thought about networking to promote themselves were more likely to feel unclean, which in turn would prime them to think of words related to cleanliness. This experimental method, known as the "Macbeth effect" in reference to Lady Macbeth's compulsive handwashing in Shakespeare's play, predicts that when people have done something wrong, they feel a need to physically cleanse themselves to clear their conscience. This effect first appeared in the social science literature in a 2017 paper by Chen-Bo Zhong and Katie Liljenquist,[2] but other researchers repeatedly were unable to replicate it.[3] In their study of the Macbeth effect, Gino and her colleagues reported a massive effect, one that could occur randomly in fewer than one in a million tries.

Ziani had doubts about the plausibility of Gino's results.[4] But when she expressed concerns about the paper to her advisers in 2018, during the third year in her program, they discouraged her from criticizing a well-known scholar like Gino. Yet the more closely Ziani examined the study, the more concerned she became. Eventually, she arrived at three conclusions:[5]

1. The paper presents serious methodological and theoretical issues, the most severe being that it is based on a psychological mechanism (the "Macbeth Effect") that has repeatedly failed to replicate.
2. The strength of evidence against the null presented in study 1 of the paper made it extremely unlikely that the result was p-hacked [note from Max: p-hacking is described in chapter 3 of this book]: It is statistically implausible to obtain such a low p-value under the null, even when using researchers' degrees of freedom.
3. Francesca Gino had many other papers that appeared equally implausible (i.e., untrustworthy psychological mechanisms leading to large effects with very low p-values).

Ziani proceeded to write up a ten-page criticism of the Gino study, which she planned to include in her dissertation. However, the three members of her dissertation committee were very upset by the criticism, and two of them refused to sign off on the dissertation if she included the passage questioning Gino's results.[6] "Academic research is like a conversation at a cocktail party," one of the advisers wrote to Ziani. "You are storming in, shouting 'you suck.'"[7]

Ziani complied with the demands of her committee members, completed her dissertation in 2020, and, disillusioned, left academia. In the spring of 2021, after relocating from Paris to Colorado, she tried to replicate the networking experiment reported by Gino and colleagues. Using a much larger sample size, she was unable to replicate Gino's results. In the process of trying, she also identified numerous aspects of Gino's data that she found to be unbelievable.[8] Ziani also came across the insurance field study allegedly collected by Ariely for our signing-first paper and identified problematic patterns in that data.⁹ She then joined with another collaborator, who has not yet gone public, and identified numerous abnormalities across other Gino–co-authored studies. Convinced there were serious problems with multiple papers published by Gino, Ziani and her collaborator turned over the evidence to Data Colada. The two informal forensic scholars teamed with Data Colada to further evaluate the evidence.

On July 15, 2021, three weeks after my Zoom call with them, the Data Colada team emailed me and my co-authors on the 2012 signing-first paper to inform us that they had evidence that the field experiment in the paper was fraudulent. Dan Ariely responded the same day, cc-ing Shu, Mazar, Gino, and me:

> Dear Leif, Joe, and Uri,
>
> First, thanks fir [sic] doing all this work
> I feel extra bad about this because Max wanted to withdraw the paper when we discovered the problem with the randomization of the field experiment, and I insisted on keeping it. In retrospect, this should have been a trigger to look more carefully at the data, which I am very sorry we didn't do.
> We will talk between us and get back to you very soon
>
> Irrationally yours,
> Dan
> danariely.com

Notice the inconsistency of this message with Ariely's claim that we had all discussed this issue with the insurance company in 2012 (see chapter 4). Later that day, Ariely sent the following voice message through email to our research team (me, Shu, Gino, and Mazar):

> Hello to everybody. . . . The first point, I should say, is that this is, if anything is wrong, it is perfectly my—my fault, and, nobody else. I was the one that was, got the connection to the, the Hartford insurance company that ran this study. . . . We gave them the instructions of what to do, and we got the data. . . . Nina and I found the original data. . . .

I appreciated that Ariely took the blame and that he said "nobody else" was to blame. However, he had never accounted for why, over the course of ten years, he had avoided my questions about the study, fought hard against retracting the 2012 paper, and repeatedly tried to bolster its strength. And I wondered on what basis he had insisted that the mileage data were correct when I first raised questions about it in 2011.

While Ariely clarified to our team that he was the only author who had been in contact with the insurance company regarding the Study 3 data, he later told BuzzFeed News that he was innocent of fraud and implied that the insurance company was responsible.[10] "I can see why it is tempting to think that I had something to do with creating the data in a fraudulent way," he said.[11] But, according to BuzzFeed, Ariely gave conflicting answers about the origins of the data file that was the basis for the analysis.[12] Later, Ariely would say that it was unfair that the media targeted him for blame when he was only the fourth author on a five-author paper.[13]

In response to Ariely's July 15 email proposing that all five authors meet online, Mazar quickly agreed. In an email the same day, I wrote: "I would only be willing to meet as a group if I first received a clear written statement of how this fraud occurred and when Dan and Nina knew about the details of the creation of the fraud. . . . I will not participate in future communications where some member(s) of the authorship group are avoiding providing full information." Mazar responded that the only data file she had ever received was the one we used for the analyses in the published 2012 paper. Gino and Shu sent separate emails saying that they also wanted clarification of how the fraud happened before they were willing to meet.

The next day, July 16, Ariely emailed:

Hello to all,

Give me a few days to try and find the original emails.

       Irrationally yours
       Dan

Two days later, Ariely emailed, "I have looked at my email and I see no records for any communications from the insurance company. This was a long time ago and sadly I don't have any of these emails."

On July 22, Gino, Shu, and I asked *PNAS* to retract our 2012 paper. Mazar and Ariely also made independent requests for retraction around the same time.

On July 28, Ariely sent an email to me and the three other co-authors that included the claim, "I'm still in the midsts [*sic*] of reaching out to various sources to gather information about the field experiment and need a bit more time before I can give you my full account of events. Hopefully in a week or so." The next day, he emailed all of us: "I am working hard to contact the relevant people and get more info. I promise to share with you and all the team what I will find as soon as I have a clear picture of what went wrong. I still have a few people at the insurance company to talk with and this is taking a bit of time." Ariely did not fulfill that promise. As in the stories documented by the Israeli television show discussed in chapter 2, Ariely remained evasive and opaque about his data collection methods.

The Data Colada post went live on August 17, 2021. It read, in part:

> In 2012, Shu, Mazar, Gino, Ariely, and Bazerman published a three-study paper in PNAS reporting that dishonesty can be reduced by asking people to sign a statement of honest intent *before* providing information (i.e., at the top of a document) rather than *after* providing information (i.e., at the bottom of a document). In 2020, Kristal, Whillans, and the five original authors published a follow-up in PNAS entitled, "Signing at the beginning versus at the end does not decrease dishonesty."

In reference to the insurance study, Data Colada wrote:

> The authors of the 2020 paper did not attempt to replicate that field experiment, but they did discover an anomaly in the data: a large difference in *baseline* odometer readings across conditions, even though those readings were collected long *before*—many months if not years before—participants were assigned to condition. . . .
>
> Our story really starts from here, thanks to the authors of the 2020 paper, who posted the data of their replication attempts *and* the data from the original 2012 paper. A team of anonymous researchers downloaded it, and discovered that this field experiment suffers from a much bigger problem than a randomization failure: There is very strong evidence that the data were fabricated.

The post then went into extensive forensic detail to provide compelling evidence that the data in Study 3 were fabricated. For example, as shown in the top chart, figure 5.1a, Data Colada showed that a typical distribution for miles driven would be bell-shaped. But as the bottom chart, figure 5.1b, shows, the data from Study 3 were strangely uniform, with an equal number of drivers driving 0–1,000 miles as 10,000–11,000 and as 49,000–50,000, with no drivers driving above 50,000.

Data Colada also provided ample evidence that the data were changed after the initial database had been created in ways that were needed for the predicted effect to be present.

Most of the media attention surrounding our paper in 2021 focused on the insurance study and Ariely.[14] Ariely continued to tell reporters that he must have received fraudulent data from the insurance company, and he never provided any useful clarification of what had happened. I believe that

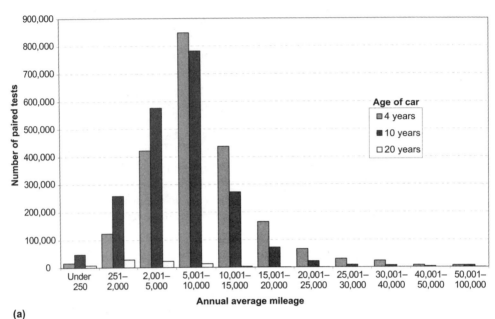

(a)

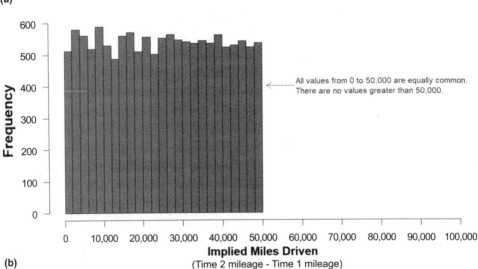

(b)

**Figures 5.1a and 5.1b**

Diagrams from Data Colada post, "Evidence of Fraud in an Influential Field Experiment About Dishonesty," August 17, 2021. Top: The data in figure 5.1a are from the UK Department for Transport, *Analysis of Vehicle Odometer Readings Recorded at MOT Tests*, June 13, 2013, available at https://bit.ly/3jwSP2N. Bottom: Figure 5.1b presents a histogram of miles driven, from L. Shu et al., "Signing at the Beginning Makes Ethics Salient and Decreases Dishonest Self-Reports in Comparison to Signing at the End," *Proceedings of the National Academy of Sciences* 109 (2012) ($N = 13{,}488$).

those I care about in my professional network did not view me with suspicion. Still, I remained uncomfortable about having my name connected to a fraudulent paper, even after voting for it to be retracted.

By this point, I also knew that Study 1—and perhaps Study 2—could not be trusted. As I mentioned in the previous chapter, Gino reported that her lab manager at her prior university managed the data collection for those two experiments. But Data Colada had shown me evidence that a similar form of research misconduct had been committed across at least four publications co-authored by Gino, which involved different co-authors and were published at very different points in time—some of them not coinciding with her employment of the North Carolina lab manager. I also knew that Data Colada, after consulting me, had decided to bring their suspicions about Gino's work to Harvard officials.

Between July 15, when Data Colada emailed our team, and July 21, I received a series of emails from Gino in which she tried to coordinate our communications to Harvard officials over the allegations against Study 3, the insurance study. This was one more problem for me. I assumed that Gino did not know at this point that Data Colada was in the process of revealing evidence against her to Harvard. I also assumed that she didn't know that I knew about potential issues with Study 1.

On July 18, Gino sent me a draft of an email she had written to Harvard officials on the allegations concerning Study 3. She proposed that I edit it and that we jointly sign it. I suggested that she add more about the replication-failure paper published in 2020. I then wrote, "Please add and send, ccing me, and then you can follow with your memo without me." I do not know if my unwillingness to sign a document with her set off alarms.

Her July 19 email to two Harvard officials, which I was copied on, read:

> I am writing to you both on behalf of my colleague Max Bazerman and I to inform you of a situation that may cast negative light on HBS and Harvard.
>
> Max and I co-authored a 2012 paper together with Lisa Shu (at a [sic] the time a doctoral student at HBS), Nina Mazar (currently at Boston University) and Dan Ariely (of Duke University). The paper was published in PNAS. Four days ago, we were informed that the data from Study 3 (a field experiment) had serious anomalies that point, quite clearly, to fraudulent data. Max, Lisa and I did not conduct that study, were not in contact with the company that ran it, and we also did not conduct the analyses on the data. This is to say that we did not touch the data, and were not involved in any part of its collection. The field experiment was conducted by an insurance company Dan Ariely was in touch

with. When he received the data, according to his account, he sent it to Nina who then analyzed it.

The people who alerted us are Uri Simonsohn, Leif Nelson, and Joe Simmons. They wrote a blogpost that will go public in the next few weeks, in their Data Colada series.

They wrote the blogpost based on re-analyses of the field data from the 2012 PNAS paper, which was made available online, on the Open Science Framework, in 2020, when we published a second paper in PNAS with a larger team of authors. The paper included studies that failed to replicate the findings demonstrated in the 2012 PNAS paper. This second paper was the result of a project Max worked on with Ariella Kristal (a current HBS doctoral student) and Ashely Whillans (a NOM colleague). When they could not replicate the findings of the 2012 PNAS paper, they invited the authors on that paper to join them on the project. The second paper was published in PNAS in 2020. As we were working on that paper, the lead author (Ariella) discovered a randomization failure in the field study, which we acknowledged in the published 2020 paper. Max and I did not conduct analyses of the field data at this point either.

Max and I both plan to write an individual memo to be posted with the blog on Data Colada. We won't read each other's memo to make sure our accounts are independent. We'll be sharing the memo with you when ready, and before it is posted.

I will also forward you both now the email trail that includes the original message from Simonsohn et al, as well as the communication that has unfolded since then. It includes an audio file in which Dan Ariely takes full responsibility for being the person who was in contact with the insurance company, received the data and shared it with Nina.

Max and I also reached out to [name redacted] and [name redacted], as they are [redacted] [note from Max: I am maintaining the confidentiality of people within Harvard] to inform them of this situation. Given the situation, we plan to retract the paper.

We are distraught given what's unfolding, and considered it important to alert you of what is going on. Please let us know what other information we can provide.

Best,

francesca

Despite what she claimed in the email, I had never authorized Gino to write to the officials on my behalf.

Four of the five authors of the 2012 paper (all but Shu) took Data Colada up on its offer to allow us to provide a written response to their posts, to be shared on the blog.[15] By July 21, I had drafted an eight-page reply that could be characterized as thorough and angry. This draft included a brief discussion of Data Colada's evidence regarding the studies collected by Gino. I shared it with Harvard officials (and not with Gino), and I received feedback from three officials. They generally encouraged me to say as little as possible, present only facts, avoid expressing anger, and avoid any mention of what I knew about Study 1. My perception was that their goal was to keep the allegations against Gino from the public until they had completed their investigation. I was also in communications with the Data Colada trio, who concurred with the Harvard officials that it would be best for the investigation into Gino if I did not mention what I had been told about Study 1.

One of the Harvard officials wrote:

Max,

I've spent 2 days reading and re-reading your statement. I am offering you feedback and suggested edits in the attached, very likely much more than you anticipated or may desire. Please know that I do this in the spirit of trying to be helpful, using [Harvard official's] "less is more" advice, trying to remain very much in the realm of fact and not opinion, and seeking to avoid language that might (inadvertently) direct blame to you when Ariely already is taking responsibility. And, while recognizing that you are angry, I tried to avoid language that felt emotional. . . .

But you will see I advocate for dropping the line that directly asserts your concerns about Studies 1 and 2. You're clear that they could not be replicated. While I understand your desire to distance yourself from them, it felt like a small bomb being dropped in this statement . . . and dropped prematurely.

I also received communications from multiple Harvard officials suggesting that leaking information about Study 1 could interfere with a possible investigation of Gino by Harvard. And I was told that if such an investigation occurred, I would not necessarily know about it, be interviewed during the process, or be provided with the results of the investigation. I inferred that this was because of concerns about due process and potential legal issues.

I found it difficult to comply with the request not to mention my concerns about Study 1 in my memo, as I wanted to be transparent. At the same time, I didn't want to interfere with a possible investigation by Harvard. The memo that I ultimately sent to Data Colada, which they posted, appears in box 5.1.

**Box 5.1**
**Evidence of Fraud in an Influential Field Experiment About Dishonesty—A Personal Reply**
Max H. Bazerman

*[This post is singly authored, without review by the other authors involved in the 2012 publication described. I want to thank Uri Simonsohn, Joe Simmons, Leif Nelson and the anonymous researchers that they mention for helping to correct the scientific record.]*

I am completely convinced by the analyses provided by Simonsohn, Simmons, and Nelson and their conclusion that the field experiment (Study 3) in Shu, Mazar, Gino, Ariely, and Bazerman (2012) contains fraudulent data; as a result, Shu, Gino, and I contacted PNAS to request retraction of the paper on July 22, 2021. I was not directly involved in the collection or statistical analysis of the data in Study 3. Nonetheless, I was a co-author of the study. It is my hope that laying out my perspective on how events unfolded will help others avoid problems in the future.

Shu, Mazar, Gino, Ariely, and Bazerman (2012) came together in a merger of two prior non-published empirical efforts. Mazar-Ariely independently provided the data for Study 3, while Shu-Gino-Bazerman had written a paper containing two laboratory experiments (Studies 1 and 2). The Shu-Gino-Bazerman group knew of the Mazar-Ariely data from multiple public presentations by Ariely. Each project appeared to respond to limitations of the other, and both projects focused on the prediction that signing before filling out a form leads to greater honesty than the traditional process of signing after.

*There were indications of problems from the start (2011).*

The first time I saw the combined three-study paper was on February 23, 2011. On this initial reading, I thought I saw a problem with implausible data in Study 3. I raised the issue with a co-author and was assured the data was accurate. I continued to ask questions because I was not convinced by the initial responses. When I eventually met another co-author responsible for this portion of the work at a conference, I was provided more plausible explanations and felt more confidence in the underlying data. I would note that this co-author quickly showed me the data file on a laptop; I did not nor did I have others examine the data more carefully.

We published the 2012 paper and it received a great deal of attention. I then believed the core result—that signing first leads to greater honesty than signing after. I presented our work in academic contexts and taught the finding to MBA and executive audiences. Multiple organizations implemented our idea of moving the signature.

**Box 5.1 (continued)**

*In 2017–2019, when we tried to replicate and extend the finding from the 2012 paper, we were unable to do so. We reported this lack of replication in two 2020 papers and backed away from the conclusions of the 2012 paper.*[16]

When I began a new project using mturk [online] experiments with Ariella Kristal and Ashley Whillans on how to induce honesty online, we started by using the "signing first" strategy as a demonstration that the existing literature provided hints on how to induce honesty. I believed that this was going to be a straightforward extension study, replicating the 2012 result in an online context.

Our first attempt did not find a difference between study participants who signed before or after, failing to provide a replication of the 2012 paper. Four additional experiments yielded the same result. We decided to do a pure, large sample size replication of the first lab experiment (Study 1). Kristal and Whillans advocated for inviting the other four authors from the original paper into the project, to make it more collaborative rather than adversarial. All four (Shu-Mazar-Gino-Ariely) agreed to join the efforts in running the large-scale pure replication, and all seven authors eventually published our paper documenting our inability to replicate the 2012 finding in PNAS as well as an article in Scientific American both explicitly rejecting the conclusion of the original study. Based on this massive failed replication project, I did my best to express my lack of confidence in any of the results in the 2012 paper in our 2020 PNAS publication.

*Our work in 2019 uncovered red flags with the field experiment, but we did not retract the paper.*

In the process of working on the 2020 paper, Kristal uncovered an unexplainably large difference in the pre-measure odometer reading (pre-treatment) between conditions, raising questions about whether a randomized experiment took place. I expressed these concerns to my co-authors and was told that the randomization failure had been discussed collectively in 2012. I have no memory of such a conversation and can find no evidence of such a conversation having included me. I would not have agreed to include the study had I known of these issues.

After the publication of the 2020 PNAS paper, PNAS raised the issue of whether the 2012 paper should be retracted. I emailed my co-authors arguing vigorously for retraction, and followed up explicitly noting the lack of randomization and the lack of transparency about the work.

> **Box 5.1 (continued)**
>
> Shu and I were the only two of the original five authors explicitly in favor of retraction, and lacking a majority we did not retract the 2012 paper. I now believe I should have independently taken action to push for retraction even without a majority of co-authors in favor of such action.
>
> In sum, I wish I had worked harder to identify the data were fraudulent, to ensure rigorous research in a collaborative context, and to promptly retract the 2012 paper. While I had doubts and raised questions, I believed the responses I received. We reported our failure to replicate the 2012 finding, but I should have argued more forcefully to retract the paper sooner.
>
> I wish to thank Ariella Kristal and Ashley Whillans for their excellent work in setting the research record straight on the signing first phenomenon, as well as Uri Simonsohn, Joe Simmons, Leif Nelson, and the anonymous researchers for all they do to help us create social science in a manner that the world can trust.
>
> **References**
>
> Shu, L., Mazar, N., Gino, F., Ariely, D, & Bazerman, M. Signing at the beginning makes ethics salient and decreases dishonest self-reports in comparison to signing at the end. Proceedings of the National Academy of Sciences, 2012, 109: 38, 15197–15200.
>
> Kristal, A.S., Whillans, A.V., Bazerman, M.H., Gino, F., Shu, L.L., Mazar, N., & Ariely, D. Signing at the beginning versus at the end does not decrease dishonesty. Proceedings of the National Academy of Sciences. 2020, 117, 7103–7107.
>
> Kristal, A.S., Whillans, A.V., Bazerman, M.H., Gino, F., Shu, L.L., Mazar, N., and Ariely, D. When we're wrong, it's our responsibility as scientists to say so. Scientific American, March 21, 2020.
>
> Sincerely,
>
> Max H. Bazerman

In the 2021 coverage of the story, the media, including social media, focused on Ariely and Study 3. Gino's role in the story stayed within Harvard until 2023. I inferred from communications with Data Colada that there were some awkward communications about information sharing between Data Colada and Harvard, but I was not involved in those discussions. I was uncomfortable about my silence about Study 1 but had made a deliberate decision not to interfere with Harvard's investigation by going public with what I knew about Study 1 and other studies by Gino that were under investigation.

For the next twenty-three months, I did not hear anything official from Harvard about the investigation of Gino. In the fall of 2021, informal channels suggested to me that something might break in a month or two, but they proved to be wrong. I spent nearly two years thinking we were a month or two from learning something about the Gino investigation.

# 6   Accusations

Both of the alleged frauds in the signing-first paper weighed heavily on my mind from the summer of 2021 until June 13, 2023. Once I decided in 2021 to maintain the secrecy of a possible investigation of Gino by Harvard, I constantly expected the investigation to end soon, only to be frustrated as more time passed. I also felt trapped by my earlier choice not to go public with what I knew in 2021.

Finally, on June 13, 2023, I received an email from a senior HBS official. It read: "I wonder whether you would have a few minutes this evening for a meeting on a confidential matter, ideally we would connect for a few minutes at 6.15pm? If that works I can send a zoom link. Best wishes, [*name redacted*]." I said yes, and the Zoom meeting was scheduled.

At 6:09, as I waited at my computer to connect to the 6:15 p.m. Zoom meeting, I received an email from a staff person at HBS informing me that HBS was recommending to *PNAS* that the existing retraction on "Signing at the Beginning Makes Ethics Salient and Decreases Dishonest Self-Reports in Comparison to Signing at the End" be amended to recognize further problems, associated with Study 1.

A fourteen-page attachment to the email documented what was being sent to *PNAS*, the journal where the 2012 paper had been published. I didn't have time to read the attachment before the 6:15 Zoom meeting. The meeting was attended by both the senior faculty official who had set it up and the staff person who had just emailed the fourteen-page attachment at 6:09 p.m. My perception was that the short call was a pleasantry aimed at clarifying that they hadn't meant to offend me with the formality of the email and attachment. I was given little additional information beyond what was in the email, with the exception that my paper with Gino was one of four papers that had been under investigation, consistent with what Data Colada had reported to me two years earlier.

During the Zoom meeting, I was told that I would soon be getting an email requesting an emergency faculty meeting of my unit at HBS for the next morning at 9 a.m. on Zoom. After the call, I received the email scheduling the meeting, an email sent to my entire unit with the exception of Francesca Gino. That evening, I thoroughly read the fourteen-page attachment, where I found the evidence that Data Colada had showed me two years earlier, supplemented by Harvard's forensic analysis of the multiple versions of the data file for Study 1 of the signing-first paper. Harvard was informing *PNAS* that its investigation had concluded that the data used in the publication of that study were fraudulent.

During the Zoom faculty meeting the next morning, June 14, many of my colleagues learned for the first time about information that I had chosen not to share with them for the prior twenty-three months. Colleagues were stunned, yet reluctant to talk about the allegations, both during and after the meeting. It was also clear that this news would create awkwardness and confusion within the department for months or years to come. In an instant, it felt as though we had changed from being one of the great management school departments in the world to a department with a big question mark attached to it.

By June 16, 2023, news stories about the scandal had begun to appear. The *Chronicle of Higher Education* reported that Gino had been placed on administrative leave without pay and would no longer be teaching or conducting research at Harvard.[1] Over the weeks that followed, the media reported that HBS dean Srikant Datar had started a process that would lead to the consideration of Gino's tenure being revoked at Harvard University. If that happened, she would be the first professor to have her tenure revoked in Harvard's long history. Gino was also banned from campus and from publishing on Harvard's publishing platforms.[2]

On June 17, 2023, Data Colada posted the evidence of fraud in Study 1 of the signing-first paper. The title of the blog post was "Clusterfake," in reference to the fact that Data Colada had already presented evidence that Study 3 of the same paper also contained fraudulent data, collected by a different author on the paper. The blog post noted that this was the first of four posts reporting allegations of fraud against Gino and that the other three posts would be coming soon. Data Colada wrote, in part:

> In 2021, we and a team of anonymous researchers examined a number of studies co-authored by Gino, because we had concerns that they contained fraudulent data. We discovered evidence of fraud in papers spanning over a decade, including papers published quite recently (in 2020).
>
> In the Fall of 2021, we shared our concerns with Harvard Business School (HBS). Specifically, we wrote a report about four studies for which we had accumulated the strongest evidence of fraud. We believe that many more Gino-authored papers contain fake data. Perhaps dozens. . . .
>
> We understand that Harvard had access to much more information than we did, including, where applicable, the original data collected using Qualtrics survey software. If the fraud was carried out by collecting real data on Qualtrics and then altering the downloaded data files, as is likely to be the case for three of these papers, then the original Qualtrics files would provide airtight evidence of fraud. (Conversely, if our concerns were misguided, then those files would provide airtight evidence that they were misguided.) . . .
>
> The evidence of fraud detailed in our report almost certainly represents a mere subset of the evidence that the Harvard investigators were able to uncover about these four articles. For example, we have heard from some HBS faculty that Harvard's internal report was ~1,200 pages long, which is 1,182 pages longer than the one we sent to HBS.[3]

The next three posts appeared on June 20, 23, and 30, each focusing on a different Gino–co-authored paper subject to allegations of data fraud.[4]

Across the four papers, Data Colada reported, it appeared as if the original data that had been entered were not sufficiently supportive of the hypothesis being studied. Then someone had reentered the database and, without a great deal of care, had made a number of changes to transform the data from not supporting the study's predictions to fully supporting them.

In its first blog post about the 2012 signing-first study, Data Colada argued that there were six rows of data that appeared to be out of order and to have been manually moved between conditions. "If this data tampering was done in a motivated fashion, so as to manufacture the desired result," the investigators wrote, "then we would expect those suspicious observations to show a particularly strong effect for the sign-on-the-top vs. sign-on-the-bottom manipulation. . . . And they do."[5] Without these data points, the predicted effect would not exist. Data Colada's evidence that the data in this study were falsified was highly convincing.

In Data Colada's second post about a Gino–co-authored paper, this one a *Psychological Science* paper published in 2015, twenty Harvard students were alleged to have filled out a demographic question about their "Year in School" with the answer "Harvard" (rather than freshman, sophomore, etc.). The Data Colada team argued that it is hard to imagine so many students made the same mistake, especially since these twenty observations all fell within thirty-five rows of data in the database. These observations also offered extreme statistical support for the predicted effect in this paper. "Without access to the original (un-tampered) data files—files we believe Harvard had access to—we can only identify instances when the data tamperer slipped up, forgetting to re-sort here, making a copy-paste error there," wrote Data Colada. "There is no reason (at all) to expect that when a data tamperer makes a mistake when changing one thing in a database, that she makes the same mistake when changing all things in that database." Without the twenty "Harvard" participants, the effect claimed to have been found in the study would not be significant.

In the third blog post in the Data Colada series, concerning a 2014 *Psychological Science* paper co-authored by Gino, once again, strange entries appear out of order in the database. And together, these unusual data points are strongly supportive of the study's prediction. Finally, in the fourth blog post about a 2020 paper Gino co-authored, there is again evidence of data tampering that created quantitative results inconsistent with the qualitative data collected by the authors. The Data Colada team limited its analyses to just four studies. But the team suggested that if Harvard opened up Gino's Qualtrics files to co-authors, many similar data anomalies might be observed.

On June 16 and 17, I emailed with Ting Zhang, Ovul Sezer, and Angus Hildreth, all then assistant professors at Harvard (Zhang) or Cornell (Sezer and Hildreth) and co-authors of papers I had published with Gino. I was trying to make sure I knew who had controlled the data in studies we had published together. I was also trying to clarify whether there was reason to trust (or not trust) papers that had Gino's name on them. This would become a broader goal of the Many Co-authors Project, which is described chapter 10.

My emails with Zhang, Sezer, and Hildreth cleared up some of my concerns, but other concerns remained. So, on June 17, to be as transparent as possible, while also seeking to clear the records of junior colleagues who might be affected by the accusations, I sent the following email to officials within HBS:

Dear colleagues:

I am writing as part of my plans to clean up the research record regarding the ethical challenges that we face. In this memo, I will address all eight of my empirical papers for which I had some concern.

As you know, there is strong evidence that the following paper should not be trusted:

Shu, L., Mazar, N., Gino, F., Ariely, D, and Bazerman, M. Signing at the beginning makes ethics salient and decreases dishonest self-reports in comparison to signing at the end. Proceedings of the National Academy of Sciences, 2012, 109: 38, 15197–15200.

I believe that the related paper should be strongly trusted, and was part of the process that led to the discovery of problems with the 2012 paper above:

Kristal, A.S., Whillans, A.V., Bazerman, M.H., Gino, F., Shu, L.L., Mazar, N., & Ariely, D. Signing at the beginning versus at the end does not decrease dishonesty. Proceedings of the National Academy of Sciences. 2020, 117, 7103–7107.

For the following three papers, I have discussed these papers with my other co-authors and we are confident that the data have integrity, and that the source of concern around data fraud is not relevant to these papers:

Sezer, O., Zhang, T., Gino, F., & Bazerman, M. (2016). Overcoming the outcome bias: making intentions matter. Organizational Behavior and Human Decision Processes, 2016, 137: 13–26.

Hildreth, J.A., Gino, F., Bazerman, M.H. Blind Loyalty? How Group Loyalty Makes Us See Evil or Engage In It. Organizational Behavior and Human Decision Processes, 2016, 132, 16–36.

Zhang, T., Fletcher, P.O., Gino, F., & Bazerman, M.H. Reducing Bounded Ethicality: How to Help Individuals Notice and Avoid Unethical Behavior. Special Issue on Bad Behavior. Organizational Dynamics, October/December 2015, 44(4): 310–317.

But, the following three papers were only analyzed by the source of existing concern, and when possible, I think HBS should pull the related Qualtrics files for further examination. Based on the results of such a review, I would potentially be interested in taking concerns to the appropriate journal.

Shu, L., Gino, F., & Bazerman, M.H. Dishonest deed, clear conscience: When cheating leads to moral disengagement and motivated forgetting. Personality and Social Psychology Bulletin, 2011, 37(3), 330–349.

Gino, F., Shu, L.L., & Bazerman, M.H. Nameless + Harmless = Blameless: When seemingly irrelevant factors influence judgment of (un)ethical behavior. Organizational Behavior and Human Decision Processes, 2010, 111(2), 102–115.

Gino, F., & Bazerman, M.H. When misconduct goes unnoticed: The acceptability of gradual erosion in others' unethical behavior. Journal of Experimental Social Psychology, 2009, 45(4), 708–719.

Neither Lisa Shu nor I saw the actual databases for these three papers.

Of course, I am available to review the processes that I have used to write this memo. And, as [*name redacted*] knows, I am in contact with Uri Simonsohn, who is likely to be starting a broader project to identify papers that should be trusted.

I am available to discuss any of this with you.

Sincerely,

Max H. Bazerman

In the weeks that followed, I had many discussions with colleagues who had also co-authored papers with Gino about how to determine whether the results of these papers were valid and how best to clear their names. I shared my email to HBS with many of these colleagues as a model of how they might communicate what they knew with their own universities.

On July 18, the International Association of Conflict Management (IACM) hosted a virtual discussion between Wharton professor Maurice Schweitzer and Uri Simonsohn regarding the unfolding crisis. Schweitzer was a Gino co-author, a central and visible member of the IACM community, and involved in discussions with other senior Gino co-authors about how to respond to the crisis. "My belief is that she did it," Simonsohn said during this discussion. "But there is no evidence. But it doesn't really matter." I understood Simonsohn to be saying that there was no direct physical evidence that Gino had committed fraud. Gino would later use Simonsohn's words as evidence that neither Data Colada nor Harvard had any reason to believe that she had committed fraud.

Only the IACM host who introduced the event, Schweitzer, and Simonsohn were visible and could speak on the Zoom meeting. But the Q&A feature was available, and it offered an emotional outlet for many. Here are a few of the comments and questions:

> "There must be legal consequences for this type of fraud to deter bad actors. If you charge money to be a keynote, the org should get that money back, for instance."
>
> "What do you do with a paper where Francesca collected one study but there are 6 other clean studies? Retraction or Expression of Concern for that one study?"
>
> "Any recommendations on how to handle old (but valuable) datasets in which the author simply cannot remember what data practices were used during collection (but knows no fraud was committed)?"
>
> "Should we be more suspicious towards Gino's frequent co-authors [some of whom, like me, Max, were on the call]?"

Both during and after this Zoom meeting, other commentators seemed to be piling on in the search for suspicious data. One blogger suggested that another Gino study had "unbelievable" data.[6] In that study, many study participants had entered the same very specific number (i.e., $150,324) to a question about what would be a fair settlement of a dispute.[7] The blogger argued that it was unbelievable that so many people would enter that specific number. But Gino had not touched the data in the study, and another author of the paper promptly clarified that study participants answered the question using a "slider," which they moved to specify their answers. The slider had options that were not round numbers. Thus, many participants who were aiming for $150,000 could end up with $150,324. Unfortunately, many people heard about the suspicious blog post on social media but did not hear the sensible explanation by Gino's co-author.

**Back to the Insurance Study**

Between the first Data Colada blog about Study 3 of the signing-first paper in 2021 and the summer of 2023, Dan Ariely had maintained that "the data were collected, entered, merged and anonymized by the [insurance] company and then sent to me. This was the data file that was used for the analysis and then shared publicly."[8] According to the *Chronicle of Higher Education*, Ariely reported to a Duke committee investigating him in 2022 that the "best suspicion I have" is that someone at The Hartford made a mistake and then tried to cover it up.[9] According to the *Chronicle*, Ariely was required by Duke to take an eight-week-long course on professionalism and integrity offered by Washington University, an ironic punishment given all that Ariely has published on the psychology of integrity. The *Chronicle* notes that the Washington University website identifies researchers who "have been investigated for noncompliance or misconduct and wish to move forward constructively" as good candidates for this program.[10]

Ariely's claim about the fraudulent data coming from The Hartford was countered on the morning of July 28, 2023, on the NPR show *Planet Money*.[11] Nick Fountain, the show's host, secured a statement from The Hartford, the insurance company that provided data to Ariely, saying that the data that were ultimately published had been fabricated.

Here is The Hartford's written statement in its entirety:

> Since this was first brought to our attention, we conducted a thorough records review and can confirm that in May 2008 we provided a small, single set of raw data to Dr. Ariely. This raw data set was related to approximately 6,000 vehicles,

far less than the number of data points in the Data Colada analysis of Dr. Ariely's 2012 study. We cannot find any record of Dr. Ariely ever discussing the initial data set with us or collaborating with us on any analysis. Dr. Ariely never sought our approval to publish our data in a study, violating our contract with him, which ran from July 2007 through December 2008. Our last email to Dr. Ariely was in February 2009. While some of the information included in the Data Colada analysis appears to have come from the raw data we provided, our review shows that the data is not the same. There appear to be significant changes made to the size, shape and characteristics of our data after we provided it and without our knowledge or consent. The Hartford is known for its ethics and integrity established over a 213-year-old history of honesty and transparency in our business activities.

Additional facts:

- **The data is not the same:** There is a significant difference between the size, shape and characteristics of our data versus the published data.
  - The number of policies and vehicles in our data is only a fraction of those in the published study data (3,756 policies/6,033 vehicles vs 13,488 policies/20,741 vehicles).
  - Though some of the data in the published study data is originally sourced from our data (i.e., certain columns of data match portions of the published study data), it is clear the data was manipulated inappropriately and supplemented by synthesized or fabricated data. Here's why:
    - At least half of the published data's initial odometer readings were derived from our data but were inappropriately manipulated by combining and redefining the initial and updated odometer readings. The other half was artificially synthesized from this data.
    - We believe the published data's updated odometer readings are the result of a randomly generated odometer change (ranging between 0 and 50,000 miles) plus the initial odometer reading.
  - The published study data includes two different fonts. All data in Calibri font can be tied to our data while all data of Cambria font appears to have been synthesized or fabricated.
- **The data tells a different story:** While the published data supports Ariely's hypothesis, our data does not.
  - The change in odometer readings in our data reflect what you would expect to see from real-life driving experience, illustrated by a bell-shaped graph, compared with the published study data, which shows a uniform distribution, as noted by Data Colada.
  - Our data does not contain a statistically significant difference between those who signed forms at the beginning and those who signed forms at

the end, so the hypothesis/conclusion around honesty for "Sign Beginning" and "Sign End" would not be warranted.

The Hartford's statement completely contradicted Ariely's insinuations about who the fraudster in the insurance study was. On a podcast a few months later, Ariely continued to deny knowledge of how the fraudulent data occurred. Ariely also continued to claim that the signing-first effect was replicable, a claim that I have never seen confirmed. In contrast, many replication efforts point to the lack of replicability.[12]

Another obvious party in the Ariely story was his employer, Duke University. Duke investigated the allegations against Ariely, but the university has a very troubled record with academic fraud. In 2019, Duke agreed to pay $112.5 million to settle a lawsuit over allegations that it submitted falsified data to obtain $200 million in federal research grants.[13] The lawsuit also alleged that Duke covered up the alleged fraud. This case had nothing to do with Ariely.

In January 2024, the *Chronicle of Higher Education* reported that Ariely claimed that Duke's investigation "concluded that he failed to adequately vet findings and maintain records from the experiment in question" but that "Duke turned up no evidence that he fabricated data."[14] Duke has not spoken publicly about the Ariely episode. In response to a request from the *Chronicle of Higher Education*, the university responded, "We are not in a position to confirm or fact-check anything on this."[15]

At a February 2024 meeting of the Duke University Academic Council, Duke administrators were anonymously asked by a faculty member(s) to "please explain why Duke is 'not in a position' to reassure the Duke community—and indeed the world—that Duke takes academic fraud seriously?" The questioner continued: "Or, better yet, could you please reconsider your determination that Duke is not able to provide any information on this matter?"[16] Jennifer Lodge, Duke's vice president for research and innovation, provided little explanation for the university's failure to meet any reasonable standard of transparency and integrity, the *Chronicle* reported. Instead, Duke simply stood behind the shield of confidentiality.[17]

Prior to this story unfolding in 2021, Ariely was the James B. Duke Professor of Psychology and Behavioral Economics at Duke University. This honorific title was no longer on his Duke website or CV in the spring of 2024, but he was still listed as a professor of business administration. With almost three years having passed since the Data Colada team reported its analysis of the insurance data, if Duke found evidence to clear Ariely, I believe that the university should have made this public. If it found evidence of wrongdoing, it has a moral obligation to Ariely's co-authors and colleagues, and the broader community, to be clear about what the university investigators know about the fraud involved in the insurance study. The failure of Duke to act with greater transparency is an embarrassment to the university's community and to academia more broadly.

# 7 The Lawsuit

On August 2, 2023, Francesca Gino announced on LinkedIn that she was suing Harvard, HBS dean Srikant Datar, and the three members of Data Colada—Simonsohn, Simmons, and Nelson—for "at least $25 million and injunctive relief." She repeated her claim that she "never, ever falsified data or engaged in research misconduct of any kind."[1] The one-hundred-page complaint, filed in the U.S. District Court in Boston, argued that Gino had been defamed by the plaintiffs and also accused Harvard of violating fair processes in its investigation and of gender discrimination by treating her more harshly than men who have also been investigated for research misconduct. The lawsuit claims that at least some of the raw data were collected on paper that no longer exists. The lawsuit fails to account for the pattern of changes to the online data that the Data Colada team observed across the four research papers.

Before the lawsuit was filed, the Data Colada team did not have access to all versions of the Qualtrics files connected to the four studies that had been accused of fraud. The team had relied on evidence of abnormalities in the final data sets that were used in the publication of these studies. While Gino argued that the original data (some of which was pen-and-paper data) no longer existed,[2] Harvard focused on multiple electronic files for each of the targeted studies that Gino had stored in Harvard's data system. Her lawsuit contained exhibits connected to the retraction notices that Harvard sent to the appropriate journals on June 13, 2023. These detailed retraction notices showed not only information that Data Colada discovered in 2021 but also what Harvard's forensic team discovered based on its access to the data files stored by Harvard connected to the four allegedly fraudulent studies. Across all four studies, the Harvard investigation found important differences between earlier and later versions of the data file. And in each case, the effects that the experiments purportedly showed became stronger from the earlier to the final version of the data file. I observed much of this myself as I carefully reviewed the data files that were available in Gino's complaint; in a September 16, 2023, Data Colada post (http://datacolada.org/114); and in Harvard's report, which the judge allowed to go public in March of 2024.

Despite this evidence, HBS professor Francis Frei was supportive of Gino, as were many of Gino's executive students and consulting clients. In a LinkedIn post, Frei wrote:

> My field is operations management. Which means we are obsessed with #process. My employer is Harvard Business School. Which has always seemed to me to be similarly obsessed with process. But after reading this complaint, my, I have great pause. And many, many questions.
>
> From my first hand observation, Francesca Gino overflows with integrity. I hope justice is served here.[3]

Also supporting Gino was Lawrence Lessig, a Harvard Law School professor, former director of the Safra Center for Ethics at Harvard, and 2016 U.S. presidential candidate:[4]

> This case will take a long time resolving. But having known Gino for almost a decade, and (though I do not represent her) having seen some of the evidence about the anomalies, I strongly urge any fair-minded soul to reserve judgment in this case. There is, in my mind, exactly zero chance that Gino manipulated any data at all; and from at least the one case that I've seen the analysis for, it is absolutely clear that the anomalous data was part of a gift card scam. (The scammer used purpose-made email addresses, submitted from IP addresses having nothing to do with Gino, on a machine unlike any Gino has ever used.) When the full evidence is revealed by her lawyers, with the benefit of third-party discovery and a serious data forensics expert, I am certain that there will be no serious doubt that Gino is innocent of the charge made against her.

However, Lessig disagreed with Gino's decision to sue the Data Colada (DC) trio:

> Gino's lawsuit, however, names DC's principals as defendants. That, in my view, is a mistake. The world needs more DC's, not fewer, and the burdens of litigation are overwhelming for everyone, especially non-profit and non-commercial sites on the web.

In contrast to the views of these Harvard scholars, the overall response from academics was harsh and very skeptical of Gino. Brian Nosek, a psychology professor at the University of Virginia and the executive director at Center for Open Science, posted on Gino's LinkedIn post:

> I have admired your work, and I found the Data Colada work to be damning for identifying fraudulent data in four of your papers. Your responses to that evidence in your lawsuit (p. 52–61) were not at all compelling about the combined evidence of data manipulation and how the claims of the paper were served by that manipulation.
>
> I would like to believe that you are innocent of fraud, but right now I do not. If you share compelling alternative explanations for how the data from each of those four papers came to be without fraud, I will publicly retract my belief that fraud occurred and apologize for ever saying that publicly. I would genuinely love to have to confront my error here.

Yoel Inbar, a professor of psychology at the University of Toronto, wrote on Gino's post:

> I don't believe we've ever met, but as a moral judgment researcher I'm familiar with a lot of your work. I think what you are doing is disgraceful.
>
> If the data are not fraudulent, you ought to be able to show that. If they are, but the fraud was done by someone else, name the person. Suing individual researchers for tens of millions of dollars is a brazen attempt to silence legitimate scientific criticism and sets a terrible example for our field.

More broadly, much of the academic community viewed the evidence against Gino's papers to be clear, but most remained silent given the litigation connected to the story.

## More Details Emerge

During this time, many of us involved in this story had heard about an in-depth article on the Ariely-Gino scandal that reporter Gideon Lewis-Kraus was writing for the *New Yorker*. Lewis-Kraus had told many people that the story would appear online on October 2 and in the print edition of the magazine on October 9. I spoke with Lewis-Kraus a few times for the article, mostly on background.

On September 26, I received a call from a vaguely familiar number with a 617 area code, the code for the Boston area, where I live and work. I was in a meeting with a student and did not pick up. I received another call from the same number a few minutes later. Concerned it could be some kind of emergency, I apologized to the student and took the call. To my surprise, it was Francesca Gino. I had not spoken to her in a very long time.

Gino told me that a *New Yorker* fact-checker had asked her about a number of issues in the working draft of Lewis-Kraus's forthcoming article and that she was trying to find out who had provided that information. In particular, she sounded upset that Lewis-Kraus knew about a 2015 HBS Faculty Review Board investigation into a research project she had been involved in. She also had heard from the fact-checker that Ariely was now suggesting she might be connected to the fraud in the insurance study (a rumor that would surface in Lewis-Kraus's article). She wanted to know if I was Lewis-Kraus's source.

I told her truthfully that I didn't recall ever seeing the Faculty Review Board report, that I had never heard a rumor of her being connected to the insurance study fraud, and that I wasn't Lewis-Kraus's source for either. Further, I told her, I was uncomfortable discussing the broader story with her, given the legal climate that had developed around it. The call ended abruptly.

On September 29, Gino sent an email to the faculty of the Negotiation, Organizations and Markets unit at HBS in which she defended her record. I learned that other groups at the school, and perhaps beyond, had received a similar email. In the three-page email, she asserted her innocence with respect to all data manipulation charges and tendered a blistering set of charges against the methods and processes used by Data Colada and Harvard. As I am not a lawyer, I will not cover the debate about these processes and will remain primarily focused on whether and how data fraud occurred.

In her September 29, 2023, email, Gino had argued that a single scammer could have accounted for all the abnormalities across the four allegedly fraudulent studies. My own reading of the available information was consistent with Harvard's position in its motion to dismiss most of her lawsuit:

> Similarly absent from the Complaint, yet obvious from the Final Report, is one of the primary defenses Plaintiff asserted, without evidence, during the investigation—that someone maliciously gained access to and tampered with her data on various password-protected devices and a private data repository over the course of several years in an elaborate attempt to frame her. The Committee found this theory highly implausible.[5]

Gino's September 29 email also provided a link to a website she had set up, www.francesca-v-harvard.org, where much of the same information she provided was posted, along with documentation of her reanalysis of the 2012 signing-first study—her attempt to defend that study from fraud accusations.[6] Gino had been circulating this last document to a smaller circle of colleagues in an attempt, I assume, to convince them of her innocence. I read this analysis for the first time on September 14.

Gino offered a number of critiques of Data Colada's methods for assessing Study 1 on the signing-first paper, primarily arguing that the investigators had cherry-picked evidence to make their accusation of fraud falsely compelling. Gino also claimed that Data Colada did not understand how data files get updated in Excel, which she said made some of their accusations against her less compelling. Gino also shifted blame to the lab manager at the University of North Carolina and to research assistant(s) who manually collected the data, even though back in 2020, when we failed to replicate this lab study (and Study 2 of the signing-first paper) seven times, Gino expressed confidence in the lab manager. Other people who knew the lab manager offered me the anonymous opinion that this person would not have had the skill needed to fabricate the data or an interest in doing so. Gino also provided no explanation for why data points added to files were typed in a different font. She similarly failed to explain how such changes occurred across different papers at different points in time with different lab managers. Nor did she explain why the changes across studies, between earlier and later versions of the digital files, so consistently and dramatically moved the data from not supporting the hypotheses to providing strong support for them.

The next day, September 30, a long piece by Noam Scheiber appeared in the *New York Times* that focused on the writer's five-hour interview with Gino.[7] The *Times* repeated Gino's argument that it was impossible for Harvard to conclude that she was guilty without having the original sheets of paper that study participants wrote on, which no longer existed. My own understanding of Data Colada's and Harvard's fraud allegations concerned changes to *digital* data files across time, not changes from the original sheets of paper collected from study participants.

Scheiber was sympathetic to Gino's claims of innocence but did not offer insight into how fraud appeared in her studies over time—across studies, colleagues, and support staff. Scheiber also noted that, because of this scandal and other documented questionable research methods by others, behavioral science had lost some credibility. The article ended with a quotation from Nobel Prize–winning psychologist Daniel Kahneman: "When I see a surprising finding, my default is not to believe it. Twelve years ago, my default was to believe anything that was surprising."

I read the *Times* article at our house in Vermont. After having lunch in Burlington, my spouse and I headed to the waterfront with our dog for a hike. As we arrived, my spouse's phone beeped with a text from a friend, telling her that the much-anticipated *New Yorker* piece had been posted online. Many people have since speculated that the *New Yorker* rushed to post its article on Gino and Ariely after seeing the long piece on Gino in the *Times*. Lewis-Kraus was much harsher toward Gino, and Ariely as well, than Scheiber had been toward Gino.[8]

Lewis-Kraus argued that there had been many hints of Gino's misconduct years before allegations were made, including an episode that involved me. He claims that Lakshmi Balachandra told me in 2012, when she was getting her PhD at Boston College and starting a faculty position at Babson College, that Gino's work was too good to be true, and that I had responded, "Oh, she's such a hard worker, you could learn a lot from her." I do not remember this conversation, but I am confident that I did not understand that Balachandra was telling me that she suspected Gino of fraud, if in fact that was her intent. At the same time, I can certainly imagine that I would have spoken highly of Gino at that time, as she was my valued colleague and friend. Even when I had concerns about the replicability of Studies 1 and 2 of the signing-first paper in 2020, I believed they might reflect problems such as errors made by research assistants or p-hacking—not data fraud.

Lewis-Kraus went on to discuss a 2015 complaint by a Harvard graduate student to Harvard administrators that Gino and another faculty member had created a hostile work environment and that Gino had repeatedly refused to share the raw data from their experiments with the student. The same student claimed that effects became stronger after Gino reanalyzed the data. According to Lewis-Kraus, Harvard concluded that all parties in the dispute had behaved poorly but that no administrative action was warranted.

Around 2012, another graduate student, not from Harvard, was working with Gino on a paper and thought that she caught Gino plagiarizing from a published paper. This student asked Gino about it, and Gino explained it away as an error that should simply be corrected. The student, however, found multiple other examples of similar plagiarism in Gino's writing.

The same student was working with Gino on a paper with multiple experiments, and described the following episode to Lewis-Kraus of the *New Yorker*:

Gino was, like, "I had an idea for an additional experiment that would tie everything together, and I already collected the data and wrote it up—here are the results." The former graduate student added, "My adviser was, like, 'Did you design the study together? No. Did you know it was going to happen? No. Has she sent you the data? No. Something off is happening here.'"

This unusual availability of data was separate from the plagiarism issues that this student observed.

After you suspect that someone has been dishonest, it is difficult to assess whether past evidence of unethical behavior was strong enough that you or others should have noticed and acted on it. Of course, in hindsight, I can question whether Gino's staggering productivity, her willingness and even eagerness to do work that is more typically done by doctoral students, and other unusual aspects of her work practices should have served as red flags. Yet, prior to 2021, I never considered the possibility of Gino engaging in data fabrication.

On October 10, 2023, Harvard submitted a motion to dismiss the defamation, conspiracy, and breach of contract claims in the lawsuit.[9] The motion to dismiss did not include the gender discrimination claim. In November 2023, Data Colada filed a parallel motion to dismiss Gino's claims against them of defamation and conspiracy with Harvard. Gino's lawyers responded by arguing that the facts in the case justified the claims made and that the legal process should move forward.

By October 2023, most empirical social scientists who had read the evidence that Data Colada provided were convinced that data fabrication had occurred in a very systematic manner. Not all were convinced, and not all supported the process that HBS followed during and after its investigation. On October 18, 2023, seven tenured HBS faculty members anonymously published an op-ed in the *Harvard Crimson*, the main student newspaper, criticizing HBS dean Datar for creating a process that they believed had not followed appropriate administrative practices. Missing from the op-ed was any statement of whether the authors believed that Gino may have fabricated data.[10]

As alluded to earlier, on March 12, 2024, the judge in the Gino-Harvard lawsuit ruled that Harvard's 1,254-page report should be made public. I thought I knew most of the story, but when I read the report, I was surprised to learn about an alleged conflict between Gino and Mazar. The report said that Gino had suggested that the data anomalies in the four studies might have occurred by chance, which many people, including me, found implausible. The report said that Gino also "asserted that an unknown actor with malicious intentions was a more plausible explanation than honest errors or intentional data falsification by herself." The report quoted Gino as saying that co-author Nina Mazar was "the most likely actor with malicious intentions." Gino also argued that Mazar had the means and motive to manipulate the data in the four studies, despite being an author on only one of them. But the report provided no evidence that Mazar had anything to do with the data fabrication. I have seen no evidence that would implicate Mazar in the data fabrication. Why would Mazar have falsified Gino's data? According to Gino, in retaliation for Gino's insufficient defense of Ariely from my criticisms about the insurance study, documented earlier in this book. According to the report, Gino claimed that Mazar had said to her, "You're going to hurt as much as I do."

After Harvard's report was made public, Mazar told the *Harvard Crimson* that she "was stunned to learn of Professor Gino's false claims about me."[11] Gino's "allegations amount to nothing but an unfortunate attempt to shift the blame and focus from her," Mazar continued. Gino's allegations of a conflict between her and Mazar surprised me. My own observation was that Gino avoided taking sides as much as possible during my email disputes with Ariely and Mazar. Yet I had always felt that when forced to make decisions, Gino had sided more with Ariely and Mazar than with me, particularly in the failure to retract the 2012 paper in 2020.

Harvard's investigators concluded that the claim that a malicious actor had hacked into Gino's accounts to frame her was not plausible. I agree with this assessment.

On April 9, 2024, the journal *Science* reported evidence suggesting that Gino may also have plagiarized passages in her two books.[12] *Science* identified about fifteen passages of text in the books, *Rebel Talent* and *Sidetracked*, that appeared to be directly lifted or rephrased from other sources, including media reports and research. In most of these cases, Gino did not cite the source text.

*Science* conducted its investigation after being tipped off by University of Montreal psychologist Erinn Acland that a book chapter co-written by Gino and Ariely, titled "Dishonesty Explained: What Leads Moral People to Act Immorally," appeared to contain material from numerous other sources, including published research articles and student theses. After Gino filed her lawsuit, Acland decided to "poke around" her work, she told *Science*. She "found apparent plagiarism in the very first sentence of the first work she assessed," according to *Science*. The journal reports:

> The sentence—"The accounting scandals and the collapse of billion-dollar companies at the beginning of the 21st century have forever changed the business landscape"—is word for word the same as a passage in a 2010 paper by the University of Washington management researcher Elizabeth Umphress and colleagues.

Gino's lawyer, Andrew Miltenberg, told *Science* that she is "steadfast in her commitment to uncovering the truth in each instance, responding decisively and correcting the record if necessary." However, as of March 2025, I am not aware of a public response by Gino to the charges.

In a May 8, 2024, post, the Data Colada team described their effort to have Gino's case against Data Colada dismissed on the basis that her legal arguments didn't hold water.[13] Gino's lawyers had filed a counterargument in response to the request for dismissal. In an April 26 hearing in Boston, the parties' attorneys each argued their case regarding Data Colada's motion to dismiss. Data Colada wrote:

> Gino's lawyers have to prove that we knew we were lying or that we were reckless. That poses something of a challenge because, amongst other things, we believe every single thing we wrote on the topic. Furthermore, the hundreds of hours of painstaking analysis that went into those blog posts doesn't scream out "reckless." So at this point, you're probably wondering *what* the Gino attorneys are arguing. We'll be honest here and say that, although we were at the hearing and listened to every word, we are not really sure. There was a moment when Gino's lawyer tried to make a point by taking one of our statements out of context and simply misquoting another. But our lawyer took care of that. They make no legitimate claim that we knew that we were lying. And that makes sense. Because we weren't.[14]

On September 11, 2024, U.S. District Court judge Myong J. Joun granted Harvard's and Data Colada's motions to dismiss the defamation charges, saying that Gino had not provided plausible evidence that Data Colada and Harvard had defamed her.[15] This effectively ended legal action against Data Colada. The judge did allow the breach of contract claim, which was based on the processes used by the university, to move forward. These decisions ended the defamation part of the lawsuit while allowing the breach of contract and gender discrimination claims against Harvard to move toward a trial.

In May 2025, the Harvard Corporation, the governing board of Harvard University, decided to strip Gino of tenure, and to end her employment at the university. By the end of May, Gino no longer appeared on the HBS website as a professor.

# 8  The Fraudsters

In June 2009, I accepted an email invitation from social psychologist Marcel Zeelenberg of Tilburg University in the Netherlands to speak at a conference in The Hague in February 2010. I knew Zeelenberg from a prior talk I had given at Tilburg and was happy to accept the invitation. The conference, led by Tilburg Institute for Behavioral Economics Research director Diederik Stapel, would connect prominent social scientists from the Netherlands and the United States with leaders in the Dutch government. The goal was to educate policymakers about recent social science research relevant to their decisions. That October, Stapel emailed me to introduce himself and to provide more detail about the conference, "Policy Challenges of Behavioral Science Research."

At the time, Zeelenberg and Stapel were among a group of prolific social psychologists in the Netherlands who published regularly in top research journals and captured the ear of the Dutch political establishment. I was honored to have been asked to speak at the conference. The academic speakers included illustrious social scientists, including David Laibson, Robert Cialdini, Barry Schwartz, and Eldar Shafir. The night before the conference kicked off, I attended a dinner with the other speakers, where I met Stapel, then forty-two years old. He came across to me as very confident and proud of having created the conference.

Stapel's career trajectory had been quite impressive and continued to be, but for only nineteen more months. Later in 2010, he was promoted to be the dean of the social and behavioral sciences faculty at Tilburg University. Then, in September 2011, Tilburg University suspended Stapel because of evidence that he had fabricated data used in his research publications.

The Stapel story unfolded after a relatively calm period on the social science fraud front. Early in the new millennium, there had been two stories of fraud involving young social psychologists. In the late 1990s, Harvard psychologist Karen Ruggiero worked on establishing a successful career studying the attitudes of women and other groups about discrimination. Soon after moving to the University of Texas at Austin, Ruggiero resigned in 2001 amid charges that she had faked research data while at Harvard. Ruggiero also retracted a *Personality and Social Psychology Bulletin* paper about status and discrimination, writing that "serious questions exist concerning the validity of the data which relate solely to my own work and which do not implicate my co-author in any way." Ruggiero admitted to fabricating data across five experiments published in two articles and to doctoring research that appeared in a third.[1] Ruggiero's downfall began when she refused to provide a graduate student with the original data from one of her studies. The student became suspicious that the data might not exist and notified Harvard, which investigated the matter. And, in 2006, Roxana Gonzalez was finishing up her dissertation at Carnegie Mellon University and had accepted a faculty position with Harvard Business School's Marketing unit when she was discovered to have altered the databases of completed studies to support the hypotheses. Gonzalez disappeared from the academic community soon after; she never started her position at HBS.[2]

Stapel was one of five prominent fraudsters in the field of research psychology in the following decade. This chapter overviews those five stories, ending with more detail on Stapel's case. Two of the fraudsters, Marc Hauser and Stapel, were identified by internal whistleblowers—younger scholars who had worked with them. Two others, Dirk Smeesters and Larry Sanna, were uncovered through the forensic work of Uri Simonsohn, a member of the Data Colada team. Finally, Brian Wansink's fraud was exposed largely as a result of a blog post he published documenting his engagement in questionable research practices. Most of these fraudsters resigned their positions and drifted away from public attention. Stapel, by contrast, chose to remain in the spotlight afterward, including writing a book on his fraudulent activities.

**Dirk Smeesters**

Dirk Smeesters was in the midst of a successful career as a marketing professor at the Rotterdam School of Management at Erasmus University in the Netherlands when he was accused of fraud.[3] His eclectic research claimed to show that messy workplaces were more effective ones, that commercials using skinny models were less effective than those with average-weight or heavier models, and that people who are thinking about death eat more candy.

In 2011, Uri Simonsohn of the Data Colada team read one of Smeesters's papers and saw data that he thought seemed too good to be true. On August 29 of that year, Simonsohn emailed Smeesters asking for his raw data, saying he believed there was a problem with it. By September 15, Smeesters claimed to have lost most of his data. Smeesters later admitted he had made mistakes in his research but said he had not fabricated data. Simonsohn said in an interview: "I shared my analyses with Smeesters, showing him that the data didn't look real, and I offered several times to explain my methods. He said he was going to re-run the study and retract the paper. That was all I heard until December, when Erasmus University Rotterdam contacted me and asked me to tell them why I was suspicious. They had started their own investigation."[4]

On January 31, 2012, Smeesters resigned from the university, citing personal reasons. According to a scientific integrity committee report from Erasmus, "The results in two of Smeesters' papers were statistically highly unlikely. Smeesters could not produce the raw data behind the findings, and told the committee that he cherry-picked the data to produce a statistically significant result. Those two papers are being retracted, and the university accepted Smeesters' resignation."[5]

"I am no Diederik Stapel," Smeesters told the Flemish newspaper *The Standard* that June.[6] In contrast, Simonsohn wrote in an email to reporter Thessa Lageman: "I am saying his data were forged. . . . There is no way the data were merely massaged. . . . Smeesters' justifications for his research data are irreconcilable with the evidence."[7]

## Lawrence Sanna

At the start of 2012, Lawrence Sanna was a professor at the University of Michigan known for his work in the area of embodied cognition, a then popular area of social psychology focusing on how the body and the environment influence the mind. Embodied cognition research had faced numerous critiques of overstated results and results that cannot be replicated.

While examining the literature on embodied cognition, Simonsohn took note of a study by Sanna that found that increasing one's perceived vertical height—for example, by ascending an escalator—positively affected one's moral values, such as leading one to behave more altruistically. "The evidence was very strong compared to the other papers and it puzzled me," Simonsohn told the journal *Nature*. "Every result was super-significant, and there were very large effects."[8] Simonsohn also noticed other unrealistic patterns in the data. In September 2012, Simonsohn sent an eight-page assessment report detailing his concerns to Sanna and two of his senior co-authors. After receiving back raw data that looked unrealistic to him, Simonsohn exchanged emails with Sanna and his co-authors throughout October in which Simonsohn offered to discuss his concerns, but eventually stopped receiving replies. (Simonsohn notes that the co-authors both said they were not involved in the data collection and that he does not suspect them of data manipulation.)

On December 5, 2011, the University of North Carolina, where Sanna worked when the papers were published, contacted Simonsohn to say it had started an inquiry into Sanna's research. Simonsohn provided UNC with the information he'd gathered. However, UNC did not make the results of its investigation public and told *Nature* that North Carolina law prevents the university from speaking about employee matters. In June 2012, a University of Michigan official notified Simonsohn that Sanna had resigned; the university also released little information about what had happened. Sanna subsequently asked the *Journal of Experimental Social Psychology* to retract three of his papers.

**Marc Hauser**

Marc Hauser was an evolutionary biologist with a tenured faculty position in the psychology department at Harvard. Hauser claimed that certain patterns detected by human infants are also detected by nonhuman primates (rhesus monkeys and cotton-top tamarins). But three junior members of his research team came to believe that Hauser's methods were fraudulent, as reported in the *Chronicle of Higher Education*.[9]

In one experiment, the research protocol called for two researchers to independently code a videotape of monkeys' behavior. Hauser and a research assistant both independently coded the tape. A second research assistant whom Hauser asked to analyze the results found that the assistant had not observed the monkeys seeing the change in pattern predicted by Hauser's research. Hauser's coding, however, showed the predicted effect, which would allow the experiment to be a publishable success. Bothered by the discrepancy, the second research assistant and a graduate student suggested to Hauser that an additional researcher should code the results; Hauser refused. After exchanging multiple emails with the assistant and grad student, Hauser wrote, "i am getting a bit pissed here. there were no inconsistencies!"[10]

The junior colleagues reviewed the tapes themselves, without Hauser's permission, and coded the results independently. They concluded that the experiment had failed: the monkeys in the video didn't react to the change in patterns. They also reviewed Hauser's coding and found that it did not reflect what they had observed on the tapes. As rumors spread about this incident, other lab members noted that they had had conflicts with Hauser in which he had allegedly reported false data and insisted on its use.

In the summer of 2007, the junior colleagues reported their evidence to Harvard officials, who launched a multiyear investigation of alleged scientific misconduct by Hauser. It took Harvard three years to conduct its investigation. After a Harvard faculty member leaked the story to the *Boston Globe* in 2010, Harvard made its findings available to the public. On August 20, 2010, the dean of Harvard's Faculty of Arts and Sciences, Michael Smith, confirmed that an internal investigation had found the fifty-year-old Hauser guilty of eight counts of scientific misconduct. Three counts involved published papers and five involved unpublished studies. Hauser resigned his position at Harvard and later released a statement saying he had made "some significant mistakes" and was "deeply sorry for the problems this case has caused to my students, my colleagues, and my university."[11]

Since Hauser had received federal funding for his research, the U.S. Department of Health and Human Services also launched an investigation and determined in 2012 that he was guilty of fabricating data, manipulating experimental results, and publishing falsified findings. Scientists criticized Harvard for lack of transparency in its investigation.[12] Harvard responded that "in cases where the government concludes scientific misconduct occurred, the federal agency makes those findings publicly available."[13]

Interestingly, while Hauser's downfall was related to the learning skills of monkeys, he was also well known for his work on morality. In 2006, Hauser published the book *Moral Minds: The Nature of Right and Wrong*.[14] And when his misconduct was discovered, he was working on a book titled *Evilicious: Why We Evolved a Taste for Being Bad*.[15]

**Brian Wansink**

Brian Wansink was a Cornell University professor well known for his work on consumer behavior. From 2007 to 2009, he was also the executive director of the U.S. Department of Agriculture's Center for Nutrition Policy and Promotion. Wansink studied people's food choices and developed strategies for improving them. Specifically, he showed how the size of the portion of food provided affects the amount consumed, research that led manufacturers to create mini-sized packaging. He also concluded from his research that people make less healthy food choices when eating with someone who is overweight than when eating with someone of average weight.

Wansink's fall from research stardom started with a blog post he published on his personal website in November 2016 in which he admitted to using questionable research practices. The standard scientific method involves specifying a hypothesis and then gathering data to test the hypothesis. By contrast, Wansink wrote that when a hypothesis of his was not confirmed, he kept on analyzing the data to test other hypotheses.[16] Tim van der Zee, a doctoral student at Leiden University in the Netherlands, stumbled upon the post and, in early 2017, went public with the results of an investigation he had conducted with two other young researchers, Jordan Anaya and Nick Brown. In the first four papers of Wansink's that they examined, they found 150 problems with data collection and analyses.[17] Although Wansink disavowed p-hacking in his 2016 blog post, he did, in fact, appear to engage in the practice. According to BuzzFeed, Wansink encouraged his students to analyze hundreds of variables in a quest for results that would "go virally big time."[18]

A subsequent internal review by Cornell identified an extensive list of faults with Wansink's work, including "misreporting of research data, problematic statistical techniques, failure to properly document and preserve research results, and inappropriate authorship," BuzzFeed reports.[19] In September 2018, Cornell apologized for Wansink's actions, removed him from his teaching and research posts, and required that he spend the rest of the 2018–19 academic year "cooperating with the university in its ongoing review of his prior research."[20] Wansink resigned from the university effective June 30, 2019.[21] The *Journal of the American Medical Association* retracted six of Wansink's papers after learning that he had not kept his original data and that Cornell could not vouch for the validity of his studies. By 2020, eighteen of Wansink's research papers had been retracted, seven others had been marked with expressions of concern, and fifteen others had had corrections made to them.[22]

## Diederik Stapel

As Stapel rose in prominence and rank in the Dutch university system, he worked with numerous younger scholars. In 2009, three junior colleagues read an unpublished Stapel manuscript that described study participants who were schoolchildren as having a mean age of nineteen, the *New York Times* reported.[23] Some students asked Stapel about this odd bit of data, and he explained it as a simple mistake. The students tentatively accepted his response but grew suspicious when Stapel later presented research that seemed too perfect during a seminar. This led three junior colleagues to check the raw data in other Stapel studies. Individually and collectively, they turned up a variety of data that didn't look as if they had been collected on actual study participants.[24] As this pattern continued, the junior colleagues became increasingly confident in their conclusion that something was wrong with the data being reported by their dean.

By 2011, one of the most skeptical of the junior colleagues was Ellen Evers, who was finishing her master's degree at Tilburg and entering its social psychology doctoral program with Stapel as her adviser. She was in regular communication with Job van Wolferen, a first-year doctoral student, and Yoel Inbar, an assistant professor of social psychology at Tilburg at that time. They started organizing the problems they saw and identified a dozen data sets that they found hard to believe, yet no specific piece of evidence was a smoking gun. In one instance, when Evers and van Wolferen congratulated another student for receiving an acceptance from a journal on a paper co-authored with Stapel, the graduate student responded that unfortunately, he didn't believe any of the data in the paper.[25]

Evers, van Wolferen, and Inbar faced a conundrum: When you have evidence that your dean has repeatedly committed fraud, to whom do you report him? Their department chair, who reported to Dean Stapel, was

Marcel Zeelenberg. Zeelenberg and Stapel had gone to graduate school together, had published research together, and were known to be best friends. (Recall that it was Zeelenberg who told me that Stapel would be inviting me to the conference in The Hague.) They were afraid that speaking to Zeelenberg might send him directly to Stapel's office. They decided to wait until they could speak to Zeelenberg in a safer environment.

At the end of August 2011, Evers and van Wolferen attended a conference in Colchester, in the UK, that Zeelenberg was attending as well. They planned to share their suspicions with Zeelenberg at the conference but "chickened out" for the first two days.[26] On the third day of the conference, Evers and van Wolferen asked Zeelenberg to meet after dinner one evening after all three of them had had more than one beer. They presented the hypothetical scenario of an academic who committed data fraud. What did he think should happen to the fraudster? they asked. If the allegations were accurate, "They should hang him from the highest tree," Zeelenberg reportedly responded.[27] Evers and van Wolferen then carefully presented their evidence that Stapel had committed data fraud across multiple projects.[28] By the time the meeting ended, at close to 3 a.m., Zeelenberg was convinced.

When Zeelenberg returned to Tilburg, he called and texted Stapel, saying he had an urgent matter to discuss. It was close to midnight, and Stapel assumed Zeelenberg was seeking advice about a personal matter. He headed over to Zeelenberg's house, just around the corner. There, Zeelenberg told Stapel that junior colleagues "suspect you have been committing academic fraud."[29] Stapel responded that high trees catch more wind, a reference to his prominence in the research community. Undaunted, Zeelenberg provided evidence. "I have to ask you if you are faking data," he eventually asked. "No, that's ridiculous," Stapel replied. "Of course not." But Stapel didn't shake Zeelenberg's confidence in the evidence provided by the junior colleagues.[30]

Zeelenberg turned over the evidence he had acquired to the university rector, Philip Eijlander, who was also Stapel's regular tennis partner. Eijlander soon met with Evers, van Wolferen, and Inbar. Next, he met with Stapel, a conversation that lasted five hours. It ended with Eijlander telling Stapel that he was not convinced of his innocence. As their conversations continued, Stapel claimed his contacts at other schools had collected the data for many of his studies. When Eijlander said he wanted to contact these schools, Stapel admitted the contacts did not exist. Soon, he also confessed his fraudulent activities to his wife.

A week later, Stapel formally confessed to the university. The university suspended him from his job and publicly announced the fraud. It was the lead news story in the Netherlands. "Overnight, Stapel went from being a respected professor to perhaps the biggest con man in academic science," the *New York Times* reported. Stapel was soon dismissed from Tilburg, and he provided substantial information about his fraudulent activities to the university's review committee.

In 2013, Stapel described the first time he says (others claim—confidentially—that the evidence is that his fraudulent activities predate this occurrence) that he committed fraud to a *New York Times* reporter. He said he was testing the idea that exposure to images of an attractive person would negatively affect one's self-image. Stapel was confident his hypothesis was true, but the actual data didn't support it. So Stapel sat at his kitchen table and began typing numbers into his computer that would produce the intended effect. A leading social psychology outlet, the *Journal of Personality and Social Psychology*, published the results in 2004. "I realized—hey, we can do this," Stapel told the *Times*.[31]

With this success, Stapel escalated his commitment to creating publishable data from scratch. He would design experiments based on interesting theory and hypotheses, then prepare all of the materials that would be needed to collect data—if data were actually collected. He told colleagues and students that he was collecting data at schools, train stations, and other places. But Stapel didn't run the studies at all; instead, he sat at his kitchen table and fabricated data. He handled the "data" for his research projects, even when it would have been more typical for doctoral students to do so. Multiple doctoral students published dissertations containing fraudulent data provided by Stapel—presumably with the intention of publishing the results in academic journals.

The three universities where Stapel had conducted (and pretended to conduct) research—the University of Amsterdam, where he was educated, and the University of Groningen and Tilburg University, where he had been employed as a professor—collaborated on a comprehensive and transparent investigation of Stapel's research. The resulting report concluded in November 2012 that Stapel had committed fraud in at least fifty-five papers and had provided fraudulent data included in ten of his students' PhD dissertations.³² The universities also blamed the field of psychology for "a general culture of careless, selective and uncritical handling of research and data."³³ Since Stapel was educated in and employed by public universities and had received about €2 million in federal funding, the Dutch government had the potential to prosecute him for his wrongdoing. In 2013, Stapel agreed to a plea deal that included 120 hours of community service and the loss of benefits he had received as a public university employee, worth about eighteen months of pay.³⁴

In response to the interim report, Stapel stated:

> I failed as a scientist. I adapted research data and fabricated research. Not once, but several times, not for a short period, but over a longer period of time. I realize that I have shocked and angered my colleagues because of my behavior. I put my field, social psychology, in a bad light. I am ashamed of it, and I deeply regret it. . . . I did not withstand the pressure to score, to publish, the pressure to get better over time. I wanted too much, too fast. In a system where there are few checks and balances, where people work alone, I took the wrong turn. I want to emphasize that the mistakes that I made were not born out of selfish ends.³⁵

We have more insight into Stapel's fraud than into the other instances discussed in this chapter for a number of reasons. First, he admitted to the fraud and participated in the investigation of his fraudulent activities. Second, the Dutch universities involved were far more public and transparent about their investigation and findings than were any of the American universities connected to the episodes of fraud documented in this book. In addition, Stapel offered his own account of the scandal in a book, *Ontsporing* (in English, *Derailed*).

I will draw on Stapel's admissions in chapter 11 when exploring why people engage in fraud. But, of course, we need to be careful when trying to learn from an admitted fraudster. As Denny Borsboom and Eric-Jan Wagenmakers write in a review of Stapel's memoir:

> The reader is never quite sure of whether Stapel's remorse is real. The last chapter—an unexpectedly beautiful, poetic description of Stapel waking up next to his wife—feeds the idea that the narrator may not be entirely trustworthy: It is composed of sentences that Stapel copies from the fiction writers Raymond Carver and James Joyce, but [he] presents them without quotes and only acknowledges the sources separately in the appendices (p. 314). This odd path to attribution is telling; the reader cannot help but wonder whether there may be yet another literary layer of deceit under the apparently candid book.³⁶

## Reason for Hope

One striking similarity across many of the stories in this chapter is how sloppy the fraudsters were in fabricating data and trying to cover their tracks. Sanna and Smeesters produced data that stood out to a smart forensic scholar, Uri Simonsohn. Hauser manipulated his data in plain sight, such that several different graduate students identified that something was wrong. Ruggiero refused to give junior colleagues access to her data, which prompted them to raise the issue with Harvard. Wansink engaged in questionable research practices with a level of openness that is shocking in retrospect. And Stapel hid his data collection from doctoral students in a manner that didn't conform to the standard production of legitimate social science.

In the current story, Gino frequently collected and analyzed the data for her experiments, sometimes with the assistance of paid research staff, leaving doctoral students out of the process. And Ariely provided data to his co-authors that did not make sense, based on simple statistics—the impossibility of drivers driving a uniform distribution of miles between 0 and 50,000—and fended off questions about peculiar aspects of the data. Nonetheless, it took years for many of these frauds to be uncovered.

It is concerning to imagine that others may be more carefully protecting their deceptive practices from discovery. However, there are a few reasons for hope. The fraudsters discussed in this chapter used different methods, yet they were all caught, and their careers ended. More recently, as we'll see in chapter 12, the rules of conducting social science are changing in ways that make it more difficult to get away with fraud. Many have shifted from viewing Simonsohn, Nelson, and Simmons with skepticism to seeing them as scholars who should be protected from the financial costs of a lawsuit by an alleged fraudster. In addition, more and more young scholars are being trained in the forensics of social science. I am hopeful that these and other changes will deter researchers from fabricating data and engaging in other forms of cheating.

Uncovering fraud will remain part of this process. I agree with Simonsohn, who told the journal *Nature*, "Some people are concerned that [exposing fraud] will damage psychology as a whole and the public will perceive an epidemic of fraud. I think that's unfounded." He continued, "We in psychology are actually trying to fix things. It would be ironic if that led to the perception that we are less credible than other sciences are."[37]

It is worth noting the difference in openness and transparency between the Stapel investigation in the Netherlands and the academic fraud cases uncovered in the United States. In the United States, the general counsel's office at a university often appears to be in charge of decision-making during an investigation of fraud. If this is accurate, it is unfortunate if legal concerns trump the transparency that can best protect co-authors, consumers of research, and the scientific record.

# 9   Co-authors and Colleagues

Francesca Gino certainly faced strong consequences from the allegations against her, in the form of a lost livelihood and reputation, but she was hardly the only person who experienced repercussions from her alleged fraud. "Much of the cost of Gino's fraud will be borne by her co-authors, of whom Gino had a total of 148 throughout her career," writes Bradford Tuckfield, one of those co-authors. "Many of them fear that association with her will tarnish their reputations and will cast doubt on the veracity and value of their publications."[1] In addition to my direct experience with Gino, I have witnessed the experiences of many of her other co-authors, many of whom are my friends, co-authors, and former advisees. Many of them cried as they told me of colleagues and university administrators who were newly suspicious of their ethics. Some doubted the veracity of the research they had published with Gino and were in the process of retracting papers from journals. Lives have been thrown into turmoil, and careers damaged and possibly ruined.

In the months after Gino's alleged fraud was exposed in 2023, I interviewed many of her co-authors for this book. To make the process more comfortable for these scholars, I did not record the interviews but instead took written notes. I gave the interviewees the opportunity to review and edit my summary of what I learned from them. Thus the information in this chapter has been approved by those I interviewed. Some were comfortable with me revealing their identities in this chapter; others were not.

I spoke to one of Gino's co-authors who discovered what they perceived to be dishonest behavior by her long before Data Colada posted its blog articles on Gino. This co-author stopped working on projects with Gino, then felt their career had been derailed after they lost the opportunity to publish this work. Others, after the alleged fraud was exposed, started to realize that they had been competing for jobs with researchers who had been using questionable research practices. Some left the field. Many of Gino's co-authors were busily auditing their jointly written papers for potential fraud. These audits included carefully reading published papers, assessing the provenance of all the data, reviewing the email history of communications between authors, trying to replicate the results of published studies, and asking their institutions to hire external parties to conduct independent reviews of their work.

These co-authors engaged in these activities to figure out whether they believed their own results, to decide whether to retract their published papers with Gino, and to vouch for their valid studies to their universities, readers of their work, and future potential employers. One group of co-authors, who assured me that Gino had not touched any of the data in the research they published with her, spent hundreds of hours documenting who controlled each of the data sets across multiple studies in multiple papers. They knew their data were clean yet still felt a need to document its integrity to others.

When I decided to write this book, some colleagues suggested it was too soon, as the effects of this story will unfold over many more years. I disagreed, believing it was important to get the story out to help the field begin to change for the better. But I decided to also explore Diederik Stapel's fraud, which was exposed back in 2011, because much more is known about it. From this older case, I thought, more conclusions could be drawn about how data fabrication affects co-authors and how to improve the field. So I reached out to co-authors of Stapel as well. I was stunned to learn what they had all been through and how much I didn't know about the story, though the Stapel story and other data-fabrication scandals had dominated my life for the past two and a half years.

## Diederik Stapel's Co-authors

### Marcel Zeelenberg

As we saw in the previous chapter, Marcel Zeelenberg was Stapel's best friend and colleague at Tilburg University. After junior colleagues shared their suspicions of Stapel's work, Zeelenberg turned in his friend to Tilburg's rector in 2011. I had read most of what had been written in English about Stapel, including Tilburg's extensive report on the fraud, Stapel's book, and many media accounts of the scandal, such as a long profile of Stapel in the *New York Times Magazine*. I had formed a positive impression of Tilburg University and the Dutch system based on what I read about their investigation of Stapel, but I was interested in getting an insider's view of the story.

Zeelenberg is a very well-published social psychologist, and I have read many of his papers, including the one he co-authored with Stapel. I have also met him a few times: first when I gave a talk at Tilburg in 2004, then at a conference in Jerusalem, and finally at the 2010 conference in The Hague, described in chapter 8. I formed a positive impression of him based on these limited interactions. I emailed him in December 2023 to ask whether I could interview him to learn about possible parallels between the 2021–2023 data fabrication story and the most famous prior story of data fraud in the social sciences—Stapel's. Zeelenberg has been relatively quiet about the scandal, so I was pleased when he agreed to meet with me via Zoom.

As you read in the prior chapter, Tilburg conducted an extensive investigation of Stapel's fraud, was transparent with the public about its findings, and finished the investigation in a little over a year. All of this sounded admirable to me—and then I heard Zeelenberg's version. What I learned from him was sad and frustrating. It was also the most interesting ninety minutes that I've spent learning about the impacts of data fabrication. While his story was very different than mine, his experience of being personally and professionally close to someone who was accused of data fabrication resonated strongly with me.

Zeelenberg had reported to Stapel when they were both at Tilburg. In 2010, Stapel became dean of social science at Tilburg; Zeelenberg was the head of the social psychology department. It was obviously difficult for Zeelenberg to turn in a close friend, but, as he told me, he felt an obligation to do so, and it was an obligation he fulfilled. Zeelenberg was asked to attend the press conference at which Tilburg University announced Stapel's actions and his confession. He declined, as he was not interested in being in the limelight.

Members of Tilburg's Levelt Committee (named for its chair, psycholinguist William Levelt)[2] interviewed Zeelenberg and other faculty and graduate students in the social psychology department about what they knew about Stapel's fraud. The investigation was heavily influenced by the law faculty at the university, and statistics professors handled more technical and forensic issues. Zeelenberg fully cooperated with the investigation but found the professors assigned to the investigation to be unpleasant and accusatory. Though he had alerted the university to Stapel's activities, Zeelenberg felt he was treated as if he were under suspicion rather than a trusted informant. His new dean, who replaced Stapel, told Zeelenberg that he would not make assumptions and would wait for the dust to settle after the investigation, and then see who was still standing.

Zeelenberg took responsibility for helping the junior members of the department psychologically cope and adjust their career plans in the wake of the news. The scandal demotivated many in the department, he told me. He believed it led some to leave the field and academia, and also led the university to devalue his department. The scandal also reduced the credibility of social science in Dutch society, which had valued it perhaps more than any other nation did. Zeelenberg described one colleague who had recently joined Tilburg with a large grant being recruited away by another Dutch university to get distance from the scandal. As Zeelenberg described the significant negative effects of the Stapel story, his sadness about these events came through—a sadness I could relate to, based on my recent experiences.

It also became clear to me that while Zeelenberg remained a productive and visible social psychologist, he did not feel valued by his own institution, and he encountered colleagues who wondered if he should have known more about Stapel's activities. Zeelenberg's interactions with Tilburg's leadership frustrated him, given that he was the one who'd provided evidence about Stapel's fraud. I asked why he was still at Tilburg, as his reputation and publication record should have made him a very attractive candidate for a senior position at other prestigious universities, including in the United States. He explained that his children and stepchildren kept him from moving to another country. He had applied for three jobs in the Netherlands and received no offers. A colleague at one of these Dutch universities told Zeelenberg that he was "contaminated."

Tilburg's Levelt Committee notes in its report that "great harm has been done to co-authors, and PhD students in particular, as a consequence of the fraud committed by Mr Stapel. . . . The people affected are hampered in their careers, such as when extending temporary contracts and applying for grants."[3] I had read this report carefully before talking to Zeelenberg. After speaking with him, I concluded that the Levelt Committee and the media that covered the Stapel story did not appreciate the level of harm created by Stapel's data fabrication and the stress imposed by the investigation that followed. Tilburg did an excellent job of identifying the magnitude of Stapel's frauds, but I think the university did a poor job of thinking through and managing the likely fallout from the investigation. Zeelenberg was a hero for his role in the Stapel story yet has suffered from his decision to fulfill his moral obligations.

**Ellen Evers**

We also met Ellen Evers, one of the whistleblowers in the Stapel story, in the previous chapter. Evers was especially brave in pursuing her doubts about Stapel, given that she was working for him and about to enter a doctoral program at Tilburg with him as an adviser. Stapel had more resources to support doctoral students than any other social psychologist at the university. When Evers and Job van Wolferen reported the evidence to Zeelenberg, it wasn't clear what would happen next. Would Zeelenberg believe the allegations of fraud? If not, how would Evers, van Wolferen, and Yoel Inbar survive in a department where Zeelenberg and Stapel were so influential? Who would be Evers's adviser after her relationship with Stapel was destroyed, or after he was no longer at Tilburg?

Fortunately, Zeelenberg did believe Evers and van Wolferen, and Zeelenberg and Inbar went on to serve as advisers for Evers and wrote papers with her. Evers was interviewed extensively by the Levelt Committee. Though she agrees with Zeelenberg that the investigators showed a degree of suspicion, Evers told me that she looks back at the Tilburg investigation positively—at least in comparison to stories of American social science frauds where universities kept evidence under wraps. She also appreciated that the Tilburg investigation assigned independent researchers to examine and clear papers that were not fraudulent, rather than leaving Stapel's co-authors to try to do this on their own.

Evers cooperated with the Levelt Committee's investigation but did not go public with her story. She decided that she would not deny her role as a whistleblower but would not seek publicity for it, either. She wanted to become known for her future research rather than for being the graduate student who turned in Stapel.

A few months after Stapel resigned in 2011, Evers was at a conference where she met Simmons, Simonsohn, and Nelson. Evers shared details of the Stapel story with what was becoming the Data Colada team. This was around the same time as the publication of what became their well-known paper on p-hacking, described in chapter 3. The researchers bonded over their concern for data integrity in the social sciences.

Evers received her doctorate from Tilburg in 2014 and moved to Philadelphia for a two-year postdoctoral research position at the Wharton School at Penn, under the supervision of Simonsohn and Simmons. After the first year, she left for a tenure-track position in marketing at the Haas School at Berkeley, where Nelson became her senior colleague. Thus, commiserating over data integrity issues after turning in Stapel may well have had a positive influence on Evers's career. She notes, bluntly yet pleasantly, that her role in the Stapel story may have also made her a more cynical scholar—which can have both advantages and disadvantages.

**Yoel Inbar**
Yoel Inbar received his PhD from Cornell in 2008 and then spent two years as a postdoctoral fellow at the Harvard Kennedy School of Government. Tilburg, with recruiting led by Stapel, hired Inbar in 2010 for a tenure-track position as an assistant professor. Part of Stapel's recruiting pitch was his assertion that he was going to transform Tilburg from a reasonably well-known Dutch university into an international center for social science research. Inbar was one of many American social scientists recruited to help meet this vision.

New to the Netherlands and Tilburg, Inbar sat in on Stapel's lab meetings, where his doctoral students and postdocs would share their results and get feedback from each other. Inbar quickly noticed two strange patterns. First, Stapel seemed to do all of the data collection, a task that normally falls to the most junior members of a research team. Second, Stapel's studies worked (that is, confirmed their hypotheses) all the time. By comparison, Inbar had studied with Tom Gilovich, a great social psychologist at Cornell, and recalled that Gilovich's studies worked about one-third of the time. How was Stapel's rate of success so high?

Inbar often worked out at the gym with doctoral student Job van Wolferen, and the two started to share observations about Stapel. Van Wolferen told Inbar that Evers had similar concerns, which led the three researchers to join forces in collecting the evidence against Stapel described in the previous chapter. This effort included Inbar initiating a new project with Stapel, who quickly "collected" the data for two experiments. When Inbar looked at the data, he found multiple patterns that did not make sense.

This became one of twelve studies in which Evers, van Wolferen, and Inbar organized evidence showing that "data" provided by Stapel did not add up. Despite Evers being the junior member of the trio of Stapel doubters, Inbar credits Evers for taking the lead in pulling together the evidence.

Both Evers and van Wolferen were young graduate students who risked angering the most important social psychologist at Tilburg with their accusations. Inbar would risk his job by turning in the accumulated evidence on the dean of social science. Aware of this, the three took the time they needed to make a strong case. While they were convinced of Stapel's guilt by January 2011, they waited until the summer of 2011 to present organized and conclusive evidence to Zeelenberg. Evers and van Wolferen did so at a conference in Colchester that Inbar did not attend.

Inbar appreciated the thoroughness of the Levelt Committee. While he agrees with Zeelenberg that they were not the most pleasant group to interact with, he valued the confidence they provided that Stapel would not be returning to Tilburg. Inbar witnessed the suffering that doctoral students went through as they retracted papers, reran studies, restarted research efforts, or quit the doctoral program. He also watched the social psychology program lose prestige and resources within the university. In 2014, Inbar accepted a new position at the University of Toronto. All of the Americans whom Stapel had recruited eventually left Tilburg in the aftermath of the investigation, Inbar told me.

Like Evers, Inbar did not hide his role in the Stapel story from friends or promote himself in the media story around the time of the investigation. It wasn't until he was discussing the replicability crisis on his own podcast in 2018 that he went public with his role in the story.[4] When Inbar learned about the Gino story, he brought up the idea of raising funds for Data Colada's legal expenses, as he is good friends with the team. He connected with Simine Vazire and Jessica Flake, also open-science-movement activists, to create a GoFundMe campaign to defend the Data Colada trio from the lawsuit filed by Gino (discussed in chapter 10).

### Marret Noordewier

One of Stapel's advisees and co-authors was Marret Noordewier.[5] She declined my interview request, saying she preferred not to focus on her personal situation. However, she was fine with me referencing an article she published in May 2023, the month before the Gino story broke, about the failure of universities to deal with the harm that fraudsters inflict on their co-authors, including herself. She wrote:

> Years of work were wasted, multiple papers were retracted and I had to deal with massive media attention, with committees and prosecutors investigating the fraud, and with my own questions about what had happened. I decided to pursue a second PhD. Not because it was required, but to "reboot" my career and find my place in academia again. . . . For years I thought that if enough time passed, I could leave this case behind. However, recently, I realized that it will not go away. To this day, the case and its consequences are part of conversations, questions, requests and any situation that involves sending my CV—to this day, it is a part of me.[6]

Unfortunately, this self-insight may well be prophetic for many of us living through the Gino story. While many of us hope that the scandal will soon be behind us, Noordewier had a different experience:

> It is only after investigations are completed and papers are retracted that one is left to deal with the fallout and what is left of their career. . . . Listing just a few examples cannot capture the true complexity of the situation, but obvious lasting effects include a damaged CV and the continuous need to explain the events and their consequences to colleagues and collaborators, conference attendees, funding institutions, grant reviewers, potential employers, students and so on. Rebuilding a career can also mean starting your research from scratch, reconsidering one's knowledge and building new research lines.[7]

**Gino's Co-authors**

Identifying the right co-authors to talk to about the Gino story was more complicated, as I know literally dozens of them. Many have been my students, co-authors, and friends. Many have avoided playing any role in media coverage of the story and didn't want to speak to me about it. Some I simply didn't contact, deciding it likely would be uncomfortable for them to share their story with me. For this reason, I avoided contacting many current and recent doctoral students that worked with Gino, despite the likelihood that they may have been the people most strongly affected by the allegations against her and Harvard's decision to not allow them access to the Qualtrics files for their own research. I spoke to many other co-authors "on background"—that is, anonymously. Others, including those I know and like, didn't respond to my email requests. Thus the profiles that follow are neither comprehensive nor representative. Rather, they provide anecdotal insights into the impact of the alleged data fabrications on Gino's co-authors.

**Julia Minson**

Julia is my colleague at the Harvard Kennedy School. As the 2023 events were unfolding, Julia was an associate professor facing a tenure decision in the 2024–25 academic year. When the crisis emerged in June 2023, Julia had co-authored five empirical journal publications with Gino—a significant percentage of Julia's twenty-five to thirty total publications. Their collaborative work had been published recently, between 2017 and 2022.

Julia was born in the Ural region of Russia and emigrated to the United States at age eleven. She was an undergraduate psychology major at Harvard and went on to get her PhD in psychology from Stanford in 2009 under the mentorship of Lee Ross. Like many excellent new doctorates in social psychology in the era after the 2008 stock market collapse and subsequent shrinking of the academic job market, Julia had limited opportunities for a tenure-track-position in 2009 and took an attractive postdoc/lecturer position at the Wharton School at Penn. While at Wharton, Julia initially found Uri Simonsohn intellectually intimidating, but they eventually became good friends. Through Simonsohn, Julia also became friends with Joe Simmons and Leif Nelson, and would regularly socialize with all three of them at professional gatherings.

Julia left Penn in 2013 for her new tenure-track faculty position at Harvard. Within a few years, she was working with Gino and others on a series of papers, including work aimed at identifying ways to encourage productive conversations between people with opposing views on politics and other hot-button issues. Across five empirical journal publications, their co-authors included various combinations of Karen Huang, Mike Yeomans, Alison Wood Brooks, Martha Jeong, Frances Chen, Charlie Dorison, and Hanne Collins. Gino was the senior member of the group, Brooks and Chen were peers of Julia, and the others were more junior scholars. For much of this work, Julia closely supervised the graduate students and research assistants who collected and analyzed the data, and Yeomans was the technical expert on natural language processing, a set of algorithms for coding the language used in conversations. Gino used her HBS budget to pay the significant research expenses of these projects. Gino also provided enthusiasm for the work of her colleagues and high-level guidance on moving the projects toward publication.

Generally, Julia viewed Gino as a positive force and was delighted to have her as a senior colleague. Gino was effusive in her praise of the team and their projects, which helped the team weather the more tedious and disheartening aspects of the research process. But even before the 2023 data-fabrication allegations became public, Julia had been frustrated by Gino's lack of reliability and intellectual engagement in their research projects. Gino made little time to meet with doctoral students, often failed to show up for meetings, canceled meetings at the last minute, and sometimes called Julia at the last minute to ask Julia to cover her teaching obligations. Gino's failure to provide adequate time to doctoral students had also created additional demands on Julia to fill in the mentoring void. Overall, however, the division of labor on the projects worked for Julia: She directed the work and mentored students, while Gino offered occasional input, paid the bills, and used her resources and connections to promote the work. Over time, Julia and Francesca became good friends, in part owing to their common experience of being female, immigrant professors with multiple children (Francesca four, Julia three). Their friendship also made their co-authorship of additional value to Julia.

Julia had heard rumors about Gino engaging in questionable research practices since 2018. When Julia passed on to Gino the disturbing rumors, Gino was upset, yet appreciative of the feedback. Gino assured Julia of her integrity, assurances that Julia wanted to believe. Gino's emotional claims of innocence, as well as her stated intention to work on fewer projects and more closely monitor her data, seemed genuine to Julia, and she went on to defend Gino to others. In Julia's mind, Gino was a sloppy researcher who pushed her students too hard for successful study results and did not supervise them closely enough. Julia never seriously considered the idea that Gino had fabricated data.

When the data-fabrication story broke in June 2023, Julia, like many of Gino's co-authors, was concerned about how others would view her own work. Julia and her co-authors carefully pinned down the provenance of all of the data across all co-authored studies with Gino and also audited who had had access to the data files throughout the research process. Julia and her colleagues were very confident that Gino had not looked at the raw data files for any of the experiments and verified that all the analyses in their published papers could be recreated from the raw data. But all of the co-authors on these studies were untenured, and they were deeply worried about how others would view their research.

As I explained in chapter 7, in late September 2023, Gino responded on her website (www.francesca-v-harvard.org) to Data Colada's analysis of the signing-first paper. Around this time, Gino reached out to some academics to try to get them to believe her claims. Whether out of fear or anger, most of Gino's colleagues avoided contact with her. This fear and anger grew after she filed her lawsuit. But Julia thought that the situation demanded thoughtful consideration of all possibilities, and she was willing to listen to Gino's claims against Data Colada and Harvard.

Julia had thoroughly followed Data Colada's work and had high levels of confidence in the team's skill and rigor. Still, she desperately wanted to believe that Data Colada had made a mistake and that Gino was innocent. Against a mountain of evidence provided by Data Colada, Julia did find a few pieces of evidence provided by Gino that she thought were potentially credible. Julia and Gino decided to ask Don Moore to attend a Zoom meeting with them where Gino could lay out her arguments. Don was uniquely qualified to join the discussion: He is an active enthusiast of the open science movement and was Gino's mentor, close friend, and co-author; plus, most scholars in his field view Don as a kind, honest, and very rigorous scholar. Julia and Don listened to Gino's arguments and found them to be less and less credible. By the end of the meeting, it was clear to all of them that without a clear explanation of how data had been fabricated across four papers, Julia and Don were more convinced than ever by Data Colada's evidence.

As I noted, Julia's core research program (much of it co-authored with Gino) focused on getting very hostile parties to interact with each other. Putting this work into practice, Julia tried to get Data Colada and Gino to meet with a mediator to talk through their differences. Julia's logic was that even if Gino was guilty of fabricating data, a mediated meeting with Data Colada might make her realize the weight of the evidence against her and decide to drop the lawsuit against Data Colada. Or perhaps it might even uncover some credible evidence of her innocence that Data Colada could corroborate.

This plan was not popular with either Gino or Data Colada, but after multiple tense conversations with both sides, Julia felt there was a possibility it might come to fruition. She went as far as finding a qualified mediator, whom she introduced to Gino. The mediation did not take place.

On September 16, 2023, the Data Colada team posted a new blog article that strengthened their allegations against Gino by using some of the tables from Harvard's investigation, previously kept private, that Gino included in her lawsuit. This new information erased any lingering doubts that Julia had about the allegations.[8] To the extent that any of Gino's claims were true, they were irrelevant to Julia's broader conclusion that Gino's papers featured large amounts of intentionally fabricated data with no credible explanation of who, other than Gino, had executed the fabrication.

Julia returned to the task of making sure that the research community, including those who might be involved in reviewing her for tenure, understood that her publications with Gino were clean and supporting the junior members of their research team, whose careers and love of research had been impacted by the fallout. This task of documenting the integrity of published work and supporting disillusioned students fell to many dozens of Gino co-authors. The co-authors faced skepticism from their colleagues about their work—both on papers that had real integrity problems and on those based entirely on high-integrity data.

**Don Moore**

In 1995, Don Moore went door-to-door at Northwestern University, where I was then a professor, looking for a research assistant position. He offered to work without pay, if necessary. I hired Don at a wage of $1,000 a month, I believe. Don was fantastic, and by the following year he had enrolled in the doctoral program at Northwestern. In April 1998, I started a very long visiting professorship at HBS, a visit from which I never returned. While I was visiting Harvard, Don, still a doctoral student at Northwestern, moved to Cambridge for a year as well. I thought Don was an amazing scholar from the beginning. Over the years, our friendship grew, as did our collaboration: We wrote many articles together, as well as two books.

As I mentioned in chapter 2, I introduced Don to Francesca Gino when her interests developed in areas close to Don's. Don was then a professor at Carnegie Mellon University (CMU), which decided to offer Gino a visiting assistant professor position from 2006 to 2008. The associate dean in charge of hiring passed on the task of negotiating with Gino to Don; the dean gave Don the initial offer to make, as well as CMU's maximum price. Don

# Co-authors and Colleagues                                      113

phoned Gino and told her he was calling to make her an offer. Don recalls her responding, "Woohoo, I accept!" Don told her that she should wait to hear the specifics of the offer and ask for more, and then they would then come to an agreement. Don essentially coached Gino to get the maximum amount he was entitled to offer.

At CMU, Don and Gino developed a close working relationship and ended up publishing four papers together between 2007 and 2013. Don never had any suspicions of fraud by Gino during this time. During her time at CMU, Gino became a good friend of the whole Moore family. Don describes Gino as fun and hard-working. From a distance, I was impressed by the role Don played in Gino's transformation from a struggling young scholar to the productive scholar that she became. She moved on to a tenure-track position at the University of North Carolina in 2008.

Around the time Don was moving from CMU to UC Berkeley, in 2010, Berkeley was also trying to recruit Gino from the University of North Carolina. She took a position at HBS instead, but her friendship with Don continued. When my relationship with Gino deteriorated (in the years before I became aware of her alleged fraud), I sensed that Don was bothered by this. While the three of us were rarely in the same place at the same time, we all had strong bonds with each other and were part of the same social-professional network.

Once at Berkeley, Don formed a close relationship with Leif Nelson and became very involved in the open science movement. I had multiple extended visits at Berkeley after Don moved there and found him to be about as strongly opinionated about the need to reform social science as Nelson was. I once noted to Don that he was extremely opinionated about the harms of p-hacking yet remained close friends with people who were rumored to be extreme p-hackers. Don responded by saying that we are all sinners. He admitted that while he rarely formed new friendships with known extreme p-hackers, he also rarely confronted his friends about the replicability of their published claims.

In 2021, when the Data Colada trio decided to pass on evidence of data fabrication across multiple Gino publications to Harvard, they wanted to check in with me to see if I would take the lead in turning the information over to Harvard (I declined) or at least tell them whom they might contact. Before doing so, they updated Don about what they had discovered, I assume in part because they knew I admired him and wanted to convince me of the validity of their forensics. When I showed up at the Zoom meeting with Data Colada, Don was there as well. After the trio presented their evidence about Gino's publications, included the signing-first paper, I asked Don whether the forensics were as compelling to him as they appeared to be to me. "Yes," he said sadly.

In 2023, Don was part of the organizing team for the Many Co-authors Project and one of the organizers and lead contributors to the GoFundMe campaign (to be discussed in the next chapter) to raise legal funds for Data Colada. As mentioned above, when Julia Minson contacted him in 2023 about Gino's efforts to convey her innocence, he agreed to meet with Julia and Gino via Zoom to make sure he wasn't missing anything. The Moore family was on vacation in Lake Tahoe, and Don got up early for the meeting to Zoom in from the hotel lobby. Julia and Don listened to Gino for two hours. By the end of the call, he told me, he was more convinced than ever of Data Colada's evidence against Gino. I have always felt that Don's experience of the Gino story was the closest to my own. We were both advisers, co-authors, and close friends of hers, yet convinced by the evidence. Don is a very positive person, yet his sadness over the story infused our December 2023 discussion.

Many of Gino's co-authors were devastated by the accusations and the uncertainties about the integrity of their work. Many co-authors spent hundreds of hours and tens of thousands of dollars running replications, with many being unable to replicate the results they had published. Don had his lab design and run replications of studies he had conducted with Gino. His lab also attempted to replicate Gino publications that did not include him as a co-author, to model appropriate scientific behavior within the lab and as a contribution to reforming social science. I cooperated with Moore's lab to review their plans for replication studies of the three papers on which I was a co-author with Gino. These are papers I identified in chapter 6, where I have uncertainty about the replicability of the work. Preliminary evidence from two of the replication studies was not supportive of the published effects, as documented at https://manycoauthors.org/.

**Scott Wiltermuth**

Scott attended Harvard as an undergraduate, worked for a number of years in the airline industry, received an MBA from INSEAD (a business school in France), and obtained a PhD from Stanford in organizational behavior in

2009. Scott's adviser at Stanford was Maggie Neale, who was my first doctoral advisee. Scott accepted a faculty position at the University of Southern California (USC) in 2009. I have known Scott since he was a graduate student, more professionally than socially.

Scott attended a talk that Gino gave about her research with Ariely, which purported to show that creativity leads to a higher likelihood of cheating. He approached her after the talk and suggested the possibility of the reverse—that cheating may lead people to be more creative. Gino and Scott quickly developed a research project based on this prediction, which led to three co-authored papers, including one of the four papers that were identified as fraudulent by Data Colada and Harvard. I spoke with Scott in early 2024 about his experience.

In 2022, Scott was a tenured associate professor at USC and under consideration for promotion to full professor. My own review of his record is that this should have been an easy positive decision. However, even candidates with very good records can be nervous about the faculty promotion process. The same year, Scott received and accepted a request from investigators at HBS to confidentially discuss one of the papers he had co-authored with Gino. During the meeting, HBS investigators told Scott that they had ethical concerns about the paper, particularly regarding the database for one of the experiments. As outlined to Scott, the concerns, having to do with the sorting of the database, seemed trivial to him. The details provided did not convey that any unethical activity had occurred. Why were they calling him? Scott wondered. He asked the Harvard investigators if they had concerns about other papers of Gino's. They declined to answer, but Scott inferred that a broader investigation was in progress. The Harvard investigators asked Scott to not tell anyone about their conversation, a request he honored. This included not telling his wife or colleagues and administrators at USC.

As part of his promotion process, Scott needed to identify his five best papers. One of the papers Scott planned to list was the one that he knew HBS was investigating. Due to his conversation with HBS, Scott did not list that paper. He felt anxious about the apparent investigation of Gino's work while his promotion process moved forward but kept silent about it.

Once the news broke about the actions Harvard was taking against Gino, Scott tried to reach out to her to discuss the story, but as of the end of 2023 they had not connected. Scott recalled that the experiments that Gino ran always worked. He also recalled asking her for access to the surveys conducted in the experiments. She gave him a reason why it wasn't possible for her to share access to the surveys or the resulting data—an experience he had never had with any other co-author. The paper that HBS investigated has been retracted, but Scott still has two other published papers with Gino. Both are multiexperiment papers where Gino collected the data on one of the studies. Like dozens of Gino's co-authors, Scott does not have access to the data she collected and is unclear on what the next steps should be for these papers.

Scott acknowledges that his role in this story is a privileged one. He works at a university that trusted his account of his work on the three papers with Gino. He was promoted at USC and already had tenure when the fraud was exposed. He is aware that many other co-authors, especially those early in their careers, have not benefited from such advantages.

### Me

I have described to you my connection to Gino in detail, but I haven't fully conveyed the impact of the alleged data fabrication on me. Now is the time. In 2021, I was devastated by the news that I received from Data Colada. I was angry at Ariely, and I felt angry, saddened, and betrayed by Gino. I was embarrassed that I had not worked harder, against the wishes of my co-authors, to retract the 2012 signing-first paper based on what we learned from the replication failures. I wanted to be as transparent as possible about what I knew but was limited by legal warnings and requests from Harvard not to interfere with the Gino investigation. I remained quiet and passed on many requests from the press. I spent almost two years waiting for Harvard's investigation to be completed so that we could reach the end of the story. I spent most of this time thinking the results of the investigation would be revealed within a couple of months. The few people who knew about the allegations against Gino asked me repeatedly whether Harvard was burying the story. I hoped not, but didn't know. Harvard did not interview me as part of its investigation. I spent my time writing a book on negotiation.[9]

When the news of Harvard's investigation of Gino broke in June 2023, I first felt relief. I underestimated the magnitude of media interest, the impact on Gino's co-authors, and how the scandal would affect the credibility of social science research. I was also frustrated that Harvard owned the data files that Gino had collected and made the decision not to release the data to Gino's co-authors. I wanted to look at the files for the papers I co-authored with Gino to find out whether I had more fraudulent papers that needed to be retracted. I was also frustrated that my university was not being as transparent as Stapel's had been. I assumed Harvard had good legal reasons for keeping quiet, particularly after Gino sued the university, but that did not eliminate my frustration.

Based on what I knew, I was not impressed by the media's portrayal of the story. At the same time, I felt sympathy for the journalists who were trying to cover it, as many of the people who knew the most about the story were keeping quiet. That was part of my motivation for writing this book—to be transparent about all I knew about the story without violating any confidentiality obligations I had to Harvard. I also felt an obligation to help restore social science research. I became obsessed with trying to figure out how I had ended up in the middle of such a sordid story. This book has been part of my cathartic response.

**Anonymous Co-authors**

As mentioned earlier, I spoke to many other co-authors of Gino who did not want to be identified in print. Yet even as they declined to participate, they provided insight into the pain caused by the allegedly fabricated data:

"I want to help you, but the painful and still unresolved nature of the situation makes me hesitate to take part."

"Thanks for reaching out and hope that you're doing alright, despite the circumstances. As you can imagine, this news has been extremely distressing for me, and mentally, I am not in a good place to talk about it. Maybe someday I will find some peace with it, and be able to support those who are most affected by this."

Other co-authors did speak with me, and when I sent them a summary of what I learned from them, they chose to not allow me to mention them by name or to tell their stories. Per my prior commitments to them, I respected those requests. I found it interesting that they had a need to talk to me but in the end did not want to go public with their stories. As this chapter only hints at, the impact of Gino's alleged frauds will take years to be fully realized and will have devastating effects for many.

# 10  Reactions and Repercussions

On August 13, 2023, I received an email from University of Melbourne professor Simine Vazire, Yoel Inbar, and McGill University professor Jessica Flake, all leaders in the open science movement. It read:

> We're organizing a GoFundMe for the Data Colada group (Leif Nelson, Joe Simmons, and Uri Simonsohn), to help raise funds for their legal defense against Professor Gino's $25 million lawsuit. We're reaching out to ask if you'd be willing to lend your name to the effort as a co-organizer of the GoFundMe. . . . We think you'd be a great person to have on board, because of your strong reputation, your steadfast commitment to the values behind this fundraiser, and your/our non-overlapping social networks.

I agreed to join this effort. Thirteen of us signed on as co-organizers of the GoFundMe, including Don Moore and Brian Nosek, whom you met earlier. Vazire, Inbar, and Flake took the lead. The first GoFundMe post went live on August 19, 2023.[1] It provided background on the story and asked for contributions to fund the legal defense of the Data Colada scholars.

> Leif Nelson, Joe Simmons, and Uri Simonsohn are professors who together publish the Data Colada blog. In June 2023, they published a series of blog posts (linked below) raising concerns about the integrity of the data in four papers co-authored by Harvard Business School (HBS) Professor Francesca Gino. They waited to publish these blog posts until after the HBS's investigation concluded, with HBS placing Professor Gino on leave and requesting retractions for the four papers. In early August 2023, Professor Gino filed a lawsuit for defamation against Harvard University, and against Leif, Joe, and Uri personally, claiming 25 million dollars in damages. Defending oneself in court is time-consuming and expensive regardless of the merits of the lawsuit—as First Amendment lawyer Ken White put it to Vox, "The process is the punishment." Targets of scientific criticism can thus use the legal system to silence their critics.
>
> At present, Leif, Joe, and Uri do not have pro bono representation. The lawyers they've spoken to currently estimate that their defense could cost anywhere

between $50,000 and $600,000 (depending on how far the lawsuit progresses). Their employers have so far only agreed to pay part of the legal fees. Defending science requires defending legitimate scientific criticism against legal bullying. That is why we are asking (with the permission of Leif, Joe, and Uri) for contributions to cover Data Colada's legal defense.

GoFundMe requires organizers to set a goal for campaigns; we set our goal at $250,000.[2] We didn't anticipate the degree to which people would want to express their view of Gino's lawsuit by donating money: Within two days, more than two thousand people had contributed. By early November, the campaign (gofundme.com/f/uhbka-support-data-coladas-legal-defense) had raised over $375,000 from more than thirty-three hundred contributors. Significant contributions came in from many leading social scientists, including Richard Thaler, Don Moore, and Mahzarin Banaji, and there were multiple donations of $10,000 or more from nonacademics. But it was the breadth of the contributions that was truly stunning, as it expressed the sentiment inside and outside the academic community.

In explaining the motivation to start the GoFundMe effort, Vazire told *Science*:

> The lawsuit felt like it had the potential to have a chilling effect on that kind of work. Maybe more than the financial support, the main value of the fundraiser was to show Data Colada—but also anyone else who might be in a role of deciding whether or not to pursue research on potential misconduct—that there is support for this.[3]

GoFundMe also allows donors to provide "words of support" along with their contributions. Here's a sampling of the nearly two hundred sentiments people offered:

**Alexandre S. Romariz:** As an academic in Brazil I recognize the importance of integrity checking, and I made this symbolic donation as a token of support for your work.

**Otto Johnson:** Integrity of research is critical. Shooting the messenger can't be tolerated.

**Mark DeBellis:** It's good that you looked for anomalies in the data and you shouldn't be attacked for doing that. Rather, you should be thanked. Sorry that this is happening to you. Hope you prevail.

**Luke Allen:** This aggression will not stand, man! Seriously, I'm glad to help defend integrity. Hope you guys can do a countersuit against that fraudster. Attempts at illicit intimidation like her lawsuit need to have consequences.

**Vicki Doner:** As a health care professional, I value what quality research has accomplished to better the lives of millions. Truthful and replicable data is critical to all research regardless of the outcomes. Many thanks to Data Colada for holding researchers accountable!

**Joseph D. Moran:** Attacking researchers because they questioned established findings, instead of based on the merits of their case, is un-scientific and has no place in our community.

**Arturs Kalnins:** I am thrilled about the tremendous response in support of smart and honest people who are unjustly accused. Stay strong! If you run out of money fighting this thing please come and ask for more. I will pitch in again and I'm sure many others here will also.

**Jeffrey I. Mensch:** Whistleblowing is an essential feature of the scientific method. This lawsuit is disgusting and needs to be opposed by everyone interested in rigorous research.

**Erica Dawson:** Data Colada have integrity. Francesca Gino does not. She needs to be held accountable.

**Adil Saribay:** I don't want other "powerful" scientists to get the message that they can bully and silence carefully conducted and fair criticism.

**Don Moore:** Science is self-correcting when scientists correct it. Thanks to Data Colada for helping uphold standards of scientific rigor and truth. That's worth supporting.

**William Ryan:** Lawsuits are not an OK response to scientific criticism.

**Quentin Andre:** Science is only self-correcting when researchers can discuss issues in published papers, without fear of retaliation. This lawsuit is an obvious attempt at silencing legitimate scientific criticism. Uri, Joe, Leif, we all stand behind you.

The contributions reflected the depth of support in the scientific community for Data Colada's work and outrage against Gino for suing them. It was clear where the vast majority of the behavioral science community stood on this dispute. On social media outlets, community members made it clear that they saw little reason to doubt the conclusions Harvard had reached about Gino's role in the fraud found across at least four of her papers.

On September 1, 2023, Data Colada published a blog thanking their supporters:

[The GoFundMe] campaign, and the outpouring of support it precipitated, represents the most affirming (and surprising) moment of our careers. It arrived at one of our most disheartening and unfamiliar moments. We are not an institution, we have no special resources, and we are not legal experts. We are, as one commentator described us, just "three relatively unknown guys." But we are now three guys being backed by thousands of others. It's a big difference.

As of this writing, the list consists of more than 2,600 donors. . . . It includes Nobel laureates, senior faculty, junior faculty, lecturers, postdocs, PhD students, and non-academics. It includes extremely wealthy people, and, most touchingly, students making just enough to get by. It includes many people who have supported our past efforts or initiatives. And, perhaps most tellingly, it also includes many people who professionally disagree with us. Those people might not always support Data Colada, but they are even less supportive of using lawsuits as a cudgel to stamp out good-faith scientific criticism.

Indeed, the popularity of the fundraising effort is not about our popularity. This is not about supporting *us*, this is about supporting a core scientific principle: our ability to seek the truth using facts and analyses. . . .

Beyond that, your response has sent a message, to us, to our universities, to each other, and to the world: It is not OK to use the legal system to punish scientists for drawing reasonable conclusions from stated facts. We don't know what is going to happen next, but we are confident that ultimately we will win this case, and that we will do so without having to pay much, if any, of our own money for our legal defense.[4]

The GoFundMe campaign was just one of the responses to the accusations against Gino. Her co-authors also organized to help make sense of the magnitude of the potential fraud.

### The Many Co-authors Project

By late June of 2023, I was in conversation with Uri Simonsohn about his interest in leading a project to survey all Gino co-authors to identify which of them had controlled the data in each study of the papers she co-authored. Don Moore (Haas School of Business at Berkeley), Julia Minson (Harvard Kennedy School), Juliana Schroeder (Haas School of Business at Berkeley), and Maurice Schweitzer (Wharton School of Business) also joined the effort. A core goal of the project was to protect the careers of more junior scholars, doctoral students, and recent PhDs, whose careers had been put at risk from their work being questioned. As these scholars looked for faculty positions or approached promotion decisions, it was too easy for universities to discount their work based on the fear of data fabrication—even when a little searching could clear the work of a specific co-author.

# Reactions and Repercussions 123

On July 18, the six of us emailed all of Gino's co-authors to launch the Many Co-authors Project. The email specified that we hoped to create a publicly available database of information on the provenance of all studies co-authored with Gino. We also hoped to create a living document to which authors could add information over time about all they knew and might learn about their studies co-authored with Gino. The Many Co-authors Project created a centralized database that gave every co-author the opportunity to indicate which studies had data contributed or handled by Gino. For those studies, they could also indicate whether the co-author ever had access to the raw data and whether the co-author currently had access to data that could be used to reproduce the results. The database of co-authors' reports is online and open access at https://manyco-authors.org. The site is searchable by author or by paper and can be updated by Gino's authors.

By mid-November, 2023, 112 of the 143 co-authors had fully completed the questionnaire. At that point, the data showed that of the 527 empirical studies in the 138 co-authored papers, Gino was not involved in the data collection in 341 of the studies (65 percent), was involved and had not shared the data with co-authors in 167 studies, and was involved and shared data with co-authors in nine studies; the project was lacking data on ten studies.

As shown in figure 10.1, Gino was in control of the data much more in the earlier stages of her publishing career (black bars) than in the later stages. She was not involved in data collection for the majority of studies that she co-authored from 2015 to 2023 (dark gray bars). For many of Gino's co-authors, the database helped reduce suspicion about their work.

## Organizations That Acted on Signing First

In chapter 4, I introduced Stu Baserman of Slice Insurance and described how I encouraged Slice to have its insurance claimants sign forms before filling out an online claim. Slice was paying me as a consultant for advice that now embarrasses me to have provided. In addition, Slice spent a significant amount of time implementing the idea of signing first. The good news is that I know of no evidence that signing first causes any harm; rather, our collective knowledge suggests that whether you sign before or after filling out a form has little to no effect on your honesty. But Slice, like other organizations that heard about the idea, spent resources on an ineffective intervention.

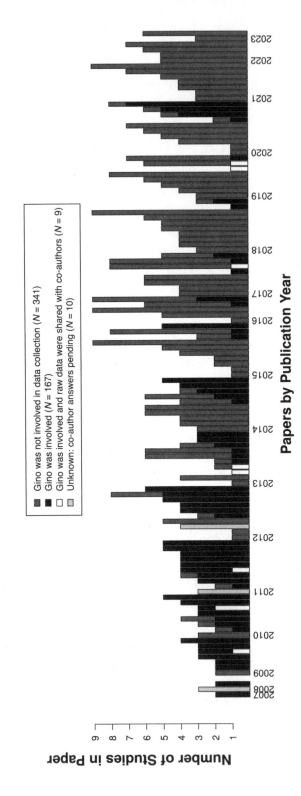

**Figure 10.1**

*Overview of all Gino-co-authored papers.* Reprinted with permission from the Many Co-Authors Project, www.manycoauthors.org. *Notes:* The figure excludes sixteen Gino co-authored articles that do not contain data. Figure is based on co-authors' self-reports. Answers were not vetted by the Many Co-authors team. An updated version of this figure may be available from https://manycoauthors.org. This version is from June 2024.

Michael Sanders from the UK Behavioural Insights Team (BIT; Nudge Unit) has spoken with understandable irritation about how the 2012 signing-first paper misdirected him, the Nudge Unit, and the Guatemalan government (see chapter 4). In addition to wasting resources, Sanders also wasted credibility convincing David Halpern, then CEO of the BIT, that signing first was a powerful tool. After learning that signing first didn't work, he had to contact Halpern, who was about to talk to the World Bank about the idea, and tell him not to do so.

Along with my co-authors on the original signing-first paper, I talked to executives about the value of signing first. The idea was well received, in part because it seemed like such an easy fix. I have no idea how many leaders wasted organizational resources implementing the idea. I feel bad about playing a role in allowing fabricated data to influence so many for so long.

**Institutional Effects**

I believe that social science, and science more broadly, creates enormous societal benefits. Scientists identify ways to help people live healthier lives. We find ways to help not-for-profit organizations thrive. We nudge people to save for a more manageable retirement. And we figure out how to educate those most in need in our society. Generally, researchers enjoy doing research that helps to make the world better. The job of figuring out what makes humans tick and how to intervene to help them make better decisions for themselves and society has been a rewarding way to spend my work life.

But the frauds discussed in this book are demoralizing, and for some, have led to despair. Syon Bhanot, a behavioral economist at Swarthmore College, told *Science* that conducting research that builds on fabricated data consumes time, energy, and resources and can leave researchers without publishable results.[5] When researchers make up their data, they may publish more easily and gain an unfair advantage as they seek job opportunities and move up the academic ladder. And, as noted earlier, many talented individuals left academia because of their inability to compete in a world where others had unfair advantages through p-hacking and fraud.

I have been a member of the Negotiation, Organizations and Markets unit of the Harvard Business School since 2000, and Gino became a member of the unit in 2010. The unit is made up of psychologists and economists who study how people make decisions and negotiate. Until 2019, I thought

I worked in the most desirable academic unit imaginable. My colleagues were fantastic, and they still are. There were many productive working relationships within the unit. We interacted openly in ways that created ideas and joy. I still like and respect my colleagues, and many remain among my closest friends. But the fabric of the unit has been damaged.

As I noted in chapter 7, while most social scientists have been convinced by the evidence of fraud provided by Data Colada, seven tenured HBS professors wrote an anonymous letter to *The Harvard Crimson* attacking HBS's investigation of Gino. Without knowing who the seven professors are, junior faculty are reluctant to discuss the data-fabrication story, as they may be unsure of the views of senior faculty who might evaluate them for promotion. Some junior faculty wonder if it is possible that Gino will somehow return as a tenured faculty member who will vote on their promotion in the future. Many of us viewed Gino as a trusted friend and colleague—a trust that has been shattered. Overall, our unit is not the place it used to be.

There is also the sense that our unit lost status within HBS. We have had a history of publishing in leading academic journals at a very high rate. Now colleagues might be asking how we did it. Was it based on honest data? Why did it take so long for Gino's data fabrication to be uncovered? Should senior colleagues like me have noticed the problem earlier? I wrote this book, in part, to address these concerns.

The harm created by Gino's alleged fraud goes far beyond her co-authors and HBS. The first two decades of the new millennium were an inspiring time for social science. The media became fascinated with our latest findings, and they shared them in ways that intrigued the public. Governments changed policies based on what we discovered. Of course, there were skeptics. Some economists continued to be anchored by the assumption that humans are perfectly rational, and they fought every result that proved that assumption wrong. There is also a growing science-denial community, which includes people who were motivated to refute evidence of the effectiveness of COVID vaccines, people who continue to believe the Earth is flat, and people who deny climate change.[6] Unfortunately, data fabrication feeds into their tendency to overgeneralize reasons to deny science, which affects public health and even the strength of our democracy.

In a guest essay in the *New York Times*, Leif Weatherby, an associate professor of German at New York University, cites the accusations against Ariely and Gino in making the following illogical conclusion:

Behavioral economics claims that humans aren't rational. That's a philosophical claim, not a scientific one, and it should be fought out in a rigorous marketplace of ideas. Instead of unearthing real, valuable knowledge of human nature, behavioral economics gives us "one weird trick" to lose weight or quit smoking.[7]

I believe that Weatherby is simply wrong in stating that the conclusion that humans aren't rational isn't a scientific claim. This is very much a valid scientific claim, one documented by many highly replicable results across many decades. The finding that signing first does not replicate should not lead society to reject the profound scientific results showing how humans depart from rationality and how we can make more rational decisions for ourselves and for society.

"Humans may not be perfectly rational, but we can do better than the predictably irrational consequences that behavioral economics has left us with today," writes Weatherby.[8] Again, he is misleading us. Behavioral economics has made great contributions to human health and has helped to improve people's savings decisions, promote more environmentally friendly acts, and increase the amount and effectiveness of charitable donations. It is tragic that the *New York Times* would publish Weatherby's misleading conclusions, but it is just one of the many repercussions of the signing-first data-fabrication story.

There was, however, some good news prompted by the scandal. As mentioned in chapter 3, Simine Vazire, one of the initiators of the GoFundMe campaign and a visible activist in the open science movement, was appointed the new editor of *Psychological Science* in January 2024. *Psychological Science* is often viewed as psychology's premier journal and was the outlet in which two of Gino's four allegedly fraudulent papers were published. In addition to the GoFundMe effort, Vazire co-founded and led the Society for the Improvement of Psychological Science, an organization that advocated for many of the reform practices I discuss in chapter 12. The appointment was an inspiration for the open science movement and a reason for hope.

# 11  Why People Cheat

Being a tenured professor at a good university is a very nice job. Teaching is an enjoyable task. Research provides us with enormous opportunity to express our creativity, and we are free to explore the ideas that interest us. And for professors at top private universities, the pay is quite good. So why would anyone risk losing such a privileged position by fabricating data?

This chapter explores that question. I discuss why rules exist, both in the world at large and in science, and why people sometimes break rules. While virtually all of us violate some rules, I will try to provide moral clarity on when breaking rules is particularly wrong and harmful. We will learn from what Diederik Stapel has told us about his frauds. And, though Ariely and Gino continue to claim their innocence, both have written extensively about when people act dishonestly and why. So we will look at what they have to say about unethical behavior as well.

**Why We Have Rules**

Perhaps you believe that it is wrong to break rules. If so, you might want to think about whether you have ever engaged in the following behaviors:

- Crossed a lightly trafficked street in the middle of the block to save the time that would be required to get to the crosswalk.
- Thrown out the junk mail sent to a previous owner or tenant of your home. (This is against the law—really!)
- Failed to get a license for your dog.
- Driven five miles per hour over the speed limit.
- Used the copier at work to make a few copies of your garage sale flier.

- Failed to pick up your dog's poop despite posted signs requiring you to do so. (After all, she pooped in the woods, and it will biodegrade, right?)

Even if you are innocent of these and other minor transgressions, I trust you can think of friends you view positively who have engaged in such behaviors or of other minor rules you have broken yourself.

Rules are made by governments, religions, families, governing bodies of sports, companies, and other groups. It is easy to recognize why we need rules, including their ability to coordinate behavior and head off chaos. Brits and Americans may have different views on whether it is better to drive on the right or the left side of the street, for example, but both groups can agree that coordinating on an answer in each country is a good idea. Similarly, agreeing on a starting time for classes and other events is helpful, even if a norm develops that these functions start seven minutes later than the formally specified time (as is true at Harvard, except at the business school, which runs on time). Through this coordination function, rules provide greater predictability and accountability for all of us.

Some people believe we should have far fewer rules and regulations than we do (I dislike lots of rules). But, to understand the benefit of rules, let's go to the extreme and imagine a world without them. In such a world, there would be no prohibitions against harming other people—no rules about slavery, child abuse, or murder. There would be no rules against cheating or stealing, either. You could drive wherever you wanted, without having your liberty limited to the right (or left) side of the road, and you wouldn't need to stop at stoplights because they wouldn't exist. Buses, trains, and airlines wouldn't have to depart at specified times, and their drivers and pilots wouldn't need training. Your organization would have no rules on when meetings or classes would start or end. Maybe not such a great idea, right? So, we need some rules!

Scientists are expected to follow rules. We follow the scientific method, which includes specifying our hypothesis before we collect data, or at least being honest about when we came up with the prediction. We have norms for what level of significance is needed to publish in our standard journals. And we certainly have rules about honesty regarding the reporting of methods and data.

In science and other realms, rules provide a fairer system that allows activities to function and survive. In the aggressive sport of American football, for example, players are not allowed to use guns or knives against their opponents—and it's hard to imagine how the game would succeed commercially without these rules.[1] The purpose of many rules is to require parties to cooperate on a solution that's better for everyone than the choices individuals would make on their own in the absence of rules. If people cannot assume that scientific data are honest, why would they believe our conclusions? The rules of science, as well as scientists' adherence to these rules, are crucial to the credibility of our contributions.

**Why We Break Rules**

Perhaps the most obvious and well-documented reason why people break rules is for selfish gain. Sometimes, individuals might be better off if they break a rule rather than follow it. This explanation lies at the core of economic theories of criminal behavior. Building on the nineteenth-century writing of philosopher Jeremy Bentham, economist Gary Becker defined the standard economic view of criminal behavior, arguing in a 1968 paper that a criminal will commit a crime when the expected benefits of doing so exceed the expected costs.[2] The kinds of benefits of rule breaking that economists consider include not only financial gains but also psychic benefits, such as prestige and self-esteem. Ariely and Gino certainly enjoyed the financial rewards and prestige of being top-tier business school professors, book writers, TED-talkers, and business consultants.

When deciding whether or not to break a rule, we might also consider the potential benefits to others, in addition to ourselves. After all, most senior researchers are concerned about their students, postdocs, and junior faculty. So let's consider this adaptation of a classic problem by Lawrence Kohlberg.[3] A woman is on her deathbed, and only one drug can save her. The drug is being sold for ten times what the drug costs to produce. The woman's partner can't afford to buy the drug and has been unsuccessful in borrowing the funds needed to purchase it. The partner breaks into a drugstore and steals the drug. In this cost-benefit analysis, the partner values the benefits of providing the drug to a loved one more than the financial costs to others and the risks of rule breaking. Many of us would find this theft on behalf of another person to be more righteous than the act of stealing to benefit ourselves financially.

Now imagine that you fell and cut your leg while walking by a café. To stop the bleeding, you grab some paper napkins from an unoccupied table without asking for permission first. Technically, this is a theft, but one that no one would blame you for committing. Of course, you could later offer to compensate the café for your use of the napkins, but that would seem silly. In this anecdote, almost everyone would agree that the benefits of the theft far outweigh the costs incurred by the restaurant owner.

People also break rules, often at significant risk to themselves, when doing so would be more moral than following them. Think of Oskar Schindler and others who violated evil Nazi laws to protect innocent people from being sent to concentration camps. In fictional movies, TV shows, and books, rule breaking is often enthusiastically endorsed when characters do so for the benefit of broader society.

Another reason people break rules is to compete against others, including those they expect are breaking the rules as well. For many years, it was very difficult to get to the top of professional baseball or cycling without using steroids, which were rampant in both sports—in part because rules against steroid use were not closely enforced. We pay attention to norms regarding whether it is acceptable to violate rules, such as driving over the speed limit, jaywalking, or taking steroids to advance in a sport. As discussed in chapter 3, prior to Data Colada's 2011 p-hacking paper, social scientists had developed a set of norms that effectively allowed for violations of the scientific method—norms that were accepted by journals, universities, and funding agencies.

How should we decide when rule breaking and other dishonest actions are allowable and even desirable? One set of relevant principles comes from utilitarian philosophy, which argues that an ethical act is one that maximizes pleasure and minimizes pain across everyone in a group or society. This goal is often stated as maximizing utility for all. Most, but not all, rules are created to maximize societal utility. So, when people create rules that benefit a small group at much larger costs to the masses, the creation of these rules can be viewed as unethical, and violating such rules may be viewed as appropriate by some.

Utilitarian views of ethical conduct illuminate why academic fraud is so wrong. A data fabricator may gain short-term personal benefits from cheating, but the harm to others is massive in comparison to these benefits. Those who commit data fraud harm their collaborators. They harm their institutions. They make people suspicious of science and thus limit the ability of useful science to improve people's lives. Collectively, the harms created by data fabrication massively outweigh the personal benefits to the fraudster. This makes these actions selfish and evil.

### Stapel on Why He Fabricated Data

In chapter 8, I described how Diederik Stapel was caught. His own account, in his book *Ontsporing* (translated as *Derailed*), provides his insights into why he did it.[4] (Keep in mind that, of course, Stapel's account is the work of an admitted fraudster.[5]) In the book, Stapel describes how he "became increasingly skilled in the use of techniques that could put a healthy looking shine on otherwise mediocre results."

> If I didn't get the effect I wanted across all the different measures I'd used or the questions I'd asked, I would use the ones that did show that effect. If an effect was present in an experiment, but not strongly enough to be tapped by all of the types of measurements I'd used, I would make it stronger by combining the measures where the effect seemed to be only partly working. If I'd designed a study for six groups of people who'd all been given slightly different tasks or shown different things and one group gave a strange result that I couldn't explain, I would change the design so that the strange result disappeared, but the whole setup still appeared coherent. Then it became a three- or four- or five-group design, instead of six. The inexplicable results went into the trash. If an experiment didn't work out, I would go hunting in the dataset for outliers (strange cases where individual participants have unexpected answers or measurements that are wildly different from the average), and look for reasons why it was OK to throw them out. If they were a little older, or younger, or slower, or faster, or in whichever way not quite "normal," then maybe it was OK to eliminate them, to bring the results more in line with what I'd been expecting.[6]

Stapel's account of his fraud is broadly consistent with the p-hacking practices that were common when his academic career developed. However, these marginal behaviors soon led to a purely fraudulent life:

> I was alone in my fancy office at University of Groningen. . . . I opened the file that contained research data I had entered and changed an unexpected 2 into a 4. . . . I looked at the door. It was closed. . . . I looked at the matrix with data and clicked my mouse to execute the relevant statistical analyses. When I saw the new results, the world had returned to being logical.

As Stapel moved from adjusting the data he collected to simply making it up, his fraudulent activities were remarkably simple and consistent:

I preferred to do it at home, late in the evening, when everyone was asleep. I made myself some tea, put my computer on the table, took my notes from my bag, and used my fountain pen to write down a neat list of research projects and effects I had to produce. . . . Subsequently I began to enter my own data, row for row, column for column. . . . 3, 4, 6, 7, 8, 4, 5, 3, 5, 6, 7, 8, 5, 4, 3, 3, 2. When I was finished, I would do the first analyses. Often, these would not immediately produce the right results. Back to the matrix and alter data. 4, 6, 7, 5, 4, 7, 8, 2, 4, 4, 6, 5, 6, 7, 8, 5, 4. Just as long until all analyses worked out as planned.[7]

Stapel compared his fraudulent behavior to an addiction:

> And like an alcoholic or a heroin addict, I began to use the object of my addiction to cope with every problem, whether that was some really bad results, or months without finding an effect, or a year without a publication, or not being able to see how to make the world a better place. I started to build a new world, my own world, from my own imagination. I twisted some of my results, and just invented some others. I did three experiments, and made up the fourth. The next time, I did one experiment and made up the other three. Then I did a whole study where I made up all of the experiments.[8]

He lists other factors that prompted his fraud, including: "The need to score, ambition, laziness, nihilism, want of power, status anxiety, desire for solutions, unity, pressure to publish, arrogance, emotional detachment, loneliness, disappointment, ADD, addiction to answers."[9]

Like many addicts, Stapel also describes many unsuccessful attempts at quitting his fraudulent behavior:

> But I can't do it. I can't escape from myself. I'm addicted. I'm a junkie. Whatever I try to get me back to regular, honest, step-by-step research, it doesn't work. I keep wanting to go faster and farther. I only want the very best. For me and for everyone around me. I'm my own little god, sitting on my throne in the depths of my soul. I can't stop; it's become automatic, a part of me. I've become conditioned by my own lies. There's no rationality, no intention, no thought process involved any more. I'd like to change, but I can't. I'm always going to need my regular hit of easy answers and perfect structures. Even if we move to another city, even if they make me the boss of a prestigious new research institute, even if I become dean of faculty, even if everyone else turns a blind eye to it.[10]

All of the accounts that I have read about Stapel suggest he cared about his students and colleagues. If this was true, how could he create so much harm for so many? *Ontsporing* provides some insight on this topic as well:

> Why did I decide to bring other people into my world of imaginary data? Because I thought it would make them happy to give them a fabulous source of truth that didn't really exist? Because I wanted them to have the clarity and simplicity that

I'd not been able to have myself? Because I wanted to help them succeed? Don't be so naïve. Isn't there a much simpler explanation? Didn't I abuse their trust for my own ends? "Stapel's published another great article. There's a guy who really knows how to look after his students."[11]

Psychologists Denny Borsboom and Eric-Jan Wagenmakers posit that trust and the lack of scientific control structures made it hard for Stapel to resist temptation.[12] Stapel says:

> Nobody ever checked my work. They trusted me. . . . I did everything myself, and next to me was a big jar of cookies. No mother, no lock, not even a lid. . . . Every day, I would be working and there would be this big jar of cookies, filled with sweets, within reach, right next to me—with nobody even near. All I had to do was take it.[13]

Stapel had become cynical of the research process and viewed academic science as becoming a business, Yudhijit Bhattacharjee reports in the *New York Times*. Stapel told the reporter:

> There are scarce resources, you need grants, you need money, there is competition. Normal people go to the edge to get that money. Science is of course about discovery, about digging to discover the truth. But it is also communication, persuasion, marketing. I am a salesman. I am on the road. People are on the road with their talk. With the same talk. It's like a circus.[14]

Stapel was also obsessed with his competition with other social psychologists that he admired, including John Cacioppo and Daniel Gilbert, according to Bhattacharjee. "They give a talk in Berlin, two days later they give the same talk in Amsterdam, then they go to London," Stapel said. "They are traveling salesmen selling their story."[15]

The Tilburg committee that investigated Stapel concluded that academic incentives encourage researchers to make their findings look better than they are.[16] The committee raised questions about the extent to which we should trust researchers and leave them alone with the "big jar of cookies" Stapel referred to in his book. The committee also concluded that social science needed to clean up its act. While readers and the media like to find a simple, single explanation for events, Stapel's personal account of his fraudulent behavior makes clear that many factors contributed to his behavior. And, notably, while Stapel's post-fraud insights are intriguing, others close to the story have confidentially told me that the evidence exists that his fraud began earlier than he claims, perhaps with his dissertation.

### Scholarly Commentary on Gino and Ariely

In chapter 9, I noted that many scholars want to distance themselves as much as possible from the alleged data fabrications of Gino and Ariely. Silence on the topic is one of the results. But a few scholars have offered insights into the allegations, including a consideration of why a famous scholar might decide to cheat.

On his blog, philosopher Eric Schwitzgebel notes that it is intriguing that, like Marc Hauser (see chapter 8),[17] Gino and Ariely were among the most prominent moral psychologists in the world. "This is a *high rate* of discovered fraud among leading moral psychology researchers, especially if we assume that most fraud goes undiscovered," Schwitzgebel writes.[18] Why might immoral behavior be particularly common among morality researchers? Schwitzgebel argues that studying ethics might negatively affect researchers' ethics. As moral psychologists observe how others break the rules, they might rationalize and justify committing such behaviors for themselves, he speculates:

> If you study dishonesty, you might be struck by the thought that dishonesty is everywhere—and then if you are tempted to be dishonest you might think "well, everyone else is doing it." I can easily imagine someone in Gino's position thinking, probably most researchers have from time to time shifted around a few rows of data to make their results pop out better. Is it really so bad if I do it too? And then once the deed has been done, it probably becomes easier, for multiple reasons, to assume that such fraud is widespread and just part of the usual academic game (grounds for thinking this might include rationalization, positive self-illusion, and using oneself as a model for thinking about others).[19]

Of course, it is worth noting that the reverse could also be true: It could be that people who are especially prone to cheating feel compelled to study dishonesty as a means of better understanding their own behavior.

Gino co-author Bradford Tuckfield (also quoted in chapter 9) argues in an article in *The American Conservative* that while it is difficult to generalize about the personality type of fraudsters, he believes they have at least one thing in common: "The common thread that unites all of these frauds is ambition. Each of them were talented enough to feed their families through honest work, but each wished for more—not just money, but power, influence, fame, and immortality."[20]

He specifically notes:

# Why People Cheat

Francesca Gino was never shy about her ambition. I remember hearing her once describe how she had felt extremely unsatisfied during her two years teaching at the University of North Carolina at Chapel Hill. Her remark shocked me—UNC is a top notch school in a beautiful place. What about it could possibly be unsatisfying?

He adds:

Amazingly, several of her verified fraudulent papers were published well after she received tenure. What more did she have to gain by adding one more little publication to her already lengthy CV? Why take the risk when she already had money, acclaim, and job security at the top of her field? Wasn't tenure at Harvard enough?

And, by 2020, Gino was one of the five highest-paid employees in the entire university.[21] But, Tuckfield theorizes, ambition "consumed Gino and denied her happiness even as she should have felt comfortable and content at the pinnacle of her field. She always wanted more, and nothing was ever enough."

## Gino and Ariely on Why People Cheat

While we might question his trustworthiness, Stapel provided us with his insights into why he committed fraud. As of this writing, Gino and Ariely both maintain their innocence. Yet their prolific publications on rule breaking provide some insight into their perspective on why people break rules. In her book *Rebel Talent*, Gino celebrates the benefits of rule breaking. Speaking of "rebels" who thrive in their fields, she writes:

They love their jobs, they break the rules, and the world is better off for it. They are rebels. . . . When we mindlessly accept rules and norms rather than questioning and constructively rebelling against them, we ultimately end up stuck and unfulfilled. As leaders, we are less effective and respected.[22]

In *Rebel Talent*, Gino focuses on prosocial examples of breaking rules, where the benefits created by rule violations outweigh any harm caused. In contrast, a great deal of her other writing focuses on dishonesty, where the harm created by rule breaking far outweighs any benefits it generates.

### Creativity

Gino and Ariely both see a link between rule breaking and creativity. Ariely celebrates dishonesty in his description of Pablo Picasso, William Shakespeare, and Steve Jobs:

Pablo Picasso once said "good artists copy, great artists steal." Throughout history, there has been no dearth of creative borrowers. William Shakespeare found his plot ideas in classical Greek, Roman, Italian and historical sources and then wrote brilliant plays based on them. Even Steve Jobs occasionally boasted that much like Picasso, Apple was shameless about stealing great ideas.[23]

In a 2012 paper they co-authored entitled "The Dark Side of Creativity: Original Thinkers Can Be More Dishonest," Gino and Ariely argue that highly creative people are more likely to be dishonest than relatively less creative people because creative individuals are better at concocting rationalizations for potential dishonesty.[24] In *Rebel Talent*, Gino writes:

> I also saw how much rule breaking is associated with innovation. I followed stories of corporate corruption and misconduct, yes, but also stories of courage. These were stories of rule breaking that brought about positive change and, in ways big and small, made the world a better place. I found myself wondering, what might we all learn from these people? What are their secrets?

In a research paper co-authored with Scott Wiltermuth and Lynne Vincent, Gino writes that in their six studies,

> people judged creative forms of unethical behavior to be less unethical than less creative forms of unethical behavior, particularly when the unethical behaviors imposed relatively little direct harm on victims. As a result of perceiving behaviors to be less unethical, people punished highly creative forms of unethical behavior less severely than they punished less-creative forms of unethical behavior.[25]

Cross-cultural experience has been repeatedly connected to more creative decision processes, but it could also have a darker side, according to Gino and her colleagues. They "propose that broad foreign experiences (i.e., experiences in multiple foreign countries) foster not only cognitive flexibility but also moral flexibility."[26]

**Competition**

Being a business school professor became a more financially rewarding job in the last couple of decades, especially for the most successful professors. Large salaries from top business schools, book contracts, and consulting opportunities were available at levels that prior generations never would have imagined. Some of those who competed for such jobs might have decided to break rules to do so. Gino's own work suggests how competition for a prize can degrade ethical behavior. In research with Celia Chui and Maryam Kouchaki, Gino writes, "We found that a larger (vs. smaller) number of competitors led participants to cheat more." In addition, "having a larger number of competitors increases expectations of the absolute number of cheaters in the competition group, which heightens perceptions that cheating is an acceptable social norm, which leads to more cheating."[27]

### Ego Boosting

In a paper co-authored with Wiley Wakeman and Celia Moore, Gino argues that unethical behavior can allow people to feel more self-confident: "Individuals who misrepresent their performance as better than it actually is boost their feelings of competence."[28] Indeed, as the authors note, Bernie Madoff once said that fraudulently claiming financial success fed his ego. The authors argue that "misrepresenting one's performance as better than it objectively is can reaffirm one's perceptions of oneself as a competent person.[29]

### Habit

In a paper written with Julia Lee, Ashley Hardin, and Bidhan Parmar, Gino notes that behaving unethically can easily become a habit. The authors write, "Cheaters were also more likely to engage in repeated unethical behavior."[30] As you'll recall, Stapel described developing a habit of cheating, one he described as addictive. The habit persisted long after he had become a famous academic. My reading of Data Colada's posts suggests that whoever fabricated the data in the four papers co-authored by Gino used a consistent habitual pattern. Specifically, unlike in Stapel's work, actual studies appear to have been run, and the data were later adjusted to make the results significant. While this pattern was very different from Stapel's, the pattern is consistent with habitual behavior.

### Overcommitment

Earlier in the book, I documented Gino's high level of career activity, which some viewed as overcommitment. The same was apparently true of Ariely.[31] This makes the following conclusion of Celia Moore and Gino interesting: "The amount we have on our plate also affects the attention we can direct toward moral decisions. When our bandwidth is subsumed by other activities, our attention to potential moral implications may be lost."[32]

### Clinical Bases of Unethical Behavior

Gino goes beyond social psychology and behavioral economics to explore the possible clinical basis of dishonesty. With Julia Lee (Cunningham),

Gino concludes that a psychopathic personality can be a predictor of cheating.[33] With Maryam Kouchaki, Gino argues that

> individuals' memories of their actions become more obfuscated over time because of the psychological distress and discomfort such misdeeds cause. . . . we show that engaging in unethical behavior produces changes in memory so that memories of unethical actions gradually become less clear and vivid than memories of ethical actions or other types of actions that are either positive or negative in valence. We term this memory obfuscation of one's unethical acts over time "unethical amnesia."[34]

In another paper, these same authors write:

> When people fail to live up to their own moral standards, this knowledge is unpleasant and threatens their self-image as honest and good. Consequently, they engage in various strategies to reduce their distress, including forgetting these memories. Such memory biases and distortions are not accidental; rather, they are motivated to support our self-concept and identity.[35]

Ariely seems to agree with the idea of false memories when he suggests that Elizabeth Holmes, who committed fraud at her company, Theranos, may have rationalized her actions and convinced herself she was telling the truth.[36]

### The Cheater's High

Gino and colleagues also describe how "unethical behavior can trigger positive affect, which we term a 'cheater's high.'" These authors continue:

> The idea that unethical behavior can trigger positive affect is consistent with many anecdotal accounts of dishonesty, theft, and fraud. These accounts include wealthy individuals who delight in shoplifting affordable goods (Seagrave, 2001), joy-riders who steal cars for the thrill (Katz, 1988), and fraudsters who revel in their misdeeds (Abagnale & Redding, 2000).[37]

### Helping Others

One of the paradoxes of these stories is that Gino's and Ariely's alleged fabrications have created great harm for many of their co-authors, yet both researchers were very well liked by most of their junior colleagues. Many of these colleagues attest to Gino and Ariely's generosity toward them and their careers. If they committed fraud, how could they have risked inflicting great harm on people they seemed to care about? Their writing is intriguing on this issue. In a paper co-written with Shahar Ayal, Gino and Ariely write:

Individuals cheat more when others can benefit from their cheating and when the number of beneficiaries of wrongdoing increases. Our results indicate that people use moral flexibility to justify their self-interested actions when such actions benefit others in addition to the self. Namely, our findings suggest that when people's dishonesty would benefit others, they are more likely to view dishonesty as morally acceptable and thus feel less guilty about benefiting from cheating.[38]

### Telling a Great Story

One interesting aspect of the data-fabrication story relates to the stories that Ariely and Gino themselves told. Both were well-known speakers and storytellers. In his *New Yorker* article on Ariely and Gino, Gideon Lewis-Kraus writes that "some believed that Ariely had always had a tortuous relationship with the truth."[39] Ariely implied that such perceptions resulted from his habit of simplifying his arguments for broad, nonscientific audiences. "Ariely said that his papers adhere to academic standards, but that he sometimes simplifies how he communicates about his work for a general audience," writes Lewis-Kraus.[40]

In his book *The (Honest) Truth About Dishonesty*, Ariely tells his version of how the signing-first paper came to be. According to him, "armed with our (laboratory) evidence that when people sign their names to some kind of pledge, it puts them in a more honest disposition, we unsuccessfully approached the IRS to implement a field experiment."[41] He claims that after the IRS rejection, "we approached an insurance company" for what would turn out to be Study 3.[42]

This timeline and accounting in Ariely's storytelling is not accurate. In fact, Ariely wasn't connected to the laboratory experiments until January 2011, after they had been conducted and written up in a working paper by Shu, Gino, and me (with the data collection occurring under Gino's supervision). In contrast, *Science* reports that "Ariely mentioned the [insurance] study in a 2008 lecture and in a 2009 Harvard Business Review piece, before the metadata indicates the Excel file was created. Ariely says he does not remember when the study was conducted."[43] He also told Planet Money, "I got the data file from the insurance company in about 2007."[44] Yet, as documented in chapter 6, The Hartford claims that they only provided the data in 2008.

In addition, Ariely and Gino have told conflicting stories about the origins of their research purporting to show that wearing counterfeit products makes people feel less legitimate, research they eventually published with

Mike Norton.⁴⁵ In *The (Honest) Truth About Dishonesty*, Ariely writes that he was inspired to explore the topic after receiving a genuine Prada overnight bag from the sponsor of a talk he gave to *Harper's Bazaar* in New York.⁴⁶ According to Ariely, as he was walking around Chinatown with the bag, he passed a woman who approached a vendor who was selling obviously counterfeit handbags. She reportedly asked the man if he had any Prada bags, and he said yes, though it was clear they both understood the bags were fakes. Ariely says he watched the woman "emerge from the shop holding her fake [Prada handbag]." According to Ariely, this experience led him to wonder "whether there were other psychological forces related to fakes that go beyond external signaling," which he claimed led to his experimental work on wearing counterfeit goods with Gino and Norton.

In contrast, in her book *Sidetracked*, Gino describes visiting a souk in Dubai with her husband, Greg, who, she says, haggled and bought a counterfeit Panerai watch for just over $100. According to Gino, "his euphoria over getting such a good deal was short-lived. By the time we got back to our car, Greg said he couldn't help but feel a bit fake while wearing the watch."⁴⁷ A few pages later, she writes:

> The signal we believe we are sending to ourselves by wearing a knockoff may not match the actual signal, and it might not be consistent with our subsequent actions. I felt this was a theory worth testing empirically before thinking carefully about its implications. And so, inspired by my visit to the souk with Greg, I teamed up with some collaborators, and we designed a simple experiment.

In sum, both Ariely and Gino claimed in their writing to have come up with the idea for the study they did with Norton on the effects of wearing counterfeit products. It is striking to me that they both felt comfortable publishing accounts claiming to be the source for the studies that they ran together, without acknowledging the other's story.

### The Complicity of the Rest of Us

One explanation for why scientists fabricate data is that for many years, it seemed unlikely they would be caught. Those in the best position to notice fraud are those who know the fraudulent work best—the co-authors of the data fabricator. Speaking for myself, I simply wasn't on the lookout for this possibility before 2021. Since I first became aware of the data fabrications in my 2012 co-authored paper, I have obsessed about how this could have happened on a paper I co-authored and what role I played in the story. As I discuss in chapter 7 of my book *Complicit*, by allowing the fraud to occur when I had the skills to detect it, I was complicit in the fraud, though I did not intentionally overlook the data fabrication and had no suspicions.

As I argue in *Complicit*, most forms of complicity with wrongdoing do not involve individuals explicitly helping people commit harm. Rather, complicity with evil is often implicit; we allow the harm to happen due to our lack of attentiveness. Dolly Chugh and I coined the term "bounded awareness" to describe the predictable mistakes that people make that prevent us from noticing or focusing on critical information that is available to us.[48] In hindsight, I argue that many co-authors (including me) in the story in this book were affected by bounded awareness. This bounded awareness in turn limits the ethicality of our actions, or what Mahzarin Banaji, Dolly, and I describe as "bounded ethicality."[49]

This book focuses on misconduct in the social sciences, but scientific fraud has been found in many other fields. In one particularly vivid episode from 2002, an internal investigation at Bell Labs found that Jan Hendrik Schön, a rising physics superstar, had committed scientific misconduct in at least sixteen cases. This led to retractions, including eight in *Science* and seven in *Nature*.[50] In this vivid episode of scientific fraud, the question of co-author responsibility was discussed. While no co-authors were directly implicated in the fraud, the American Physical Society revised its code of ethics to more strongly emphasize the responsibility of collaborators.[51] However, these responsibilities have remained unclear in the scientific community. And what are the obligations of colleagues, research assistants, and supervisors who have hints that something seems off? I will return to the topic of scientific complicity in the next chapter.

In chapter 2, I detailed my relationships with key actors in the data-fabrication story and the trust I put in the work of others, as I have throughout my career. Having experienced this terrible episode, I have reached a different view on trusting my co-authors. I am still in favor of trusting others to do parts of our shared work, but I now feel an obligation to carefully verify what they do. I don't plan on publishing papers in the future without looking at the databases and doing some basic checks on the reasonableness of the data. Had I done this on the signing-first paper, I do not think my name would have ended up on a paper that Data Colada aptly called a "clusterfake."[52]

I have written elsewhere about the moral obligation of auditors to change their structures so that they are less financially incentivized to keep their clients happy by accepting questionable practices surrounding their financial reporting.[53] Given the current crisis in the social sciences, I encourage all co-authors to develop new standard practices that protect themselves and the field. In my next and final chapter, we will explore these proposed practices in detail.

# 12  Moving Forward

It would be nice if all researchers acted completely honestly and transparently and if no one engaged in p-hacking or data fabrication. This would help restore credibility to the field of psychology and the social sciences more broadly, and allow journals and universities to avoid having to put new regulations in place to prevent cheating. Of course, this is simply wishful thinking; action is needed. Restoring integrity and credibility to social science will come with costs. Many of us are currently incurring the costs of the data-fabrication stories covered in this book, in the form of suspicion about our work, time spent repeating the same story, working to put in place new safeguards to protect the integrity of our work, and dealing with the stress of the story. It is frustrating to incur these costs imposed by the unethical actions of others.

One paradoxical aspect of this book is that the core frauds that we have analyzed occurred in research focused on how to change behavior, and this chapter (and the book more broadly) is about how to change the behavior of researchers in the future. Much of the behavioral economics literature examines how to change the behavior of individuals. In contrast, Nick Chater and George Loewenstein argue that, far too often, those in power focus our attention on the need for change at the individual level (i-frame), which distracts us from making system-level changes (s-frame).[1] Combining my experience in this story, the many ideas from the open science movement, and my expertise as an organizational scholar, I will identify possible changes to the research process at both individual and system levels.

Psychology is in crisis, and whether we like it or not, we need to change how we conduct our research. Relying on Data Colada to find evidence of fraud after it has occurred is not the most useful process for preventing fraud in the future. Activists in the open science movement have outlined steps that can help repair the field. I endorse these changes, which are described in the next section. After reviewing them, I go on to discuss the role of research collaborators, journals, universities, funding agencies, and government in moving us toward a more credible field of psychology and social science.

**Moving Toward Open Science**

The Data Colada team open their 2018 paper, "Psychology's Renaissance," by writing that if a research psychologist had hibernated between 2011 and 2018, they would be shocked upon waking up to see how their field had evolved.[2] The changes the team notes include authors voluntarily posting their data online, journals publishing replication projects, researchers preregistering their studies, labs teaming up for replication projects that go through a review process by a journal before the data are even collected, and psychologists showing great interest in symposiums and articles on research methods.[3] These steps have moved us in the right direction, and more positive changes continue to be made. More is needed, however.

Just as it is unlikely there will ever be a system that leads all citizens to pay their taxes honestly, it is unlikely that we will fully eliminate p-hacking and fraud. We can do much more to reduce their incidence, however. With a focus on p-hacking, Nelson, Simmons, and Simonsohn argue for two changes to the research process: disclosure and preregistration.[4]

The basic idea behind disclosure is that any reader or reviewer should be able to fully understand what the researcher did at each stage of the research process. When did the researcher specify their hypothesis? A research paper should describe all the conditions of the experiment and all the measurements collected. The paper should also provide a clear understanding of the complete experience of experimental participants in all experimental conditions.

The need for disclosure seems obvious, yet it has been lacking in the field. One counterforce to disclosure has been readers' preferences for shorter versions of research reports. *Psychological Science* became popular and high status in part because it offered readers a much more concise write-up of experiments than typical psychology journals. When I am reading outside my primary areas of research, I appreciate being able to quickly consume short research articles. But one downside of the shorter presentation is that descriptions of research methods get squeezed out, thus reducing disclosure. Some journals have responded to this concern by moving some of the information that should be disclosed online. Such supplemental materials give willing readers the chance to devote their time to reviewing the methods in detail. Unfortunately, many of us lack the interest to do so and simply rely on the less fully disclosed presentation in the actual journal.

The Data Colada trio note that many more authors are providing disclosures, even in journals where it is not required.[5] They credit this evolution in part to the Center for Open Science for providing a suggested request that reviewers can make part of their reviews:

> I request that the authors add a statement to the paper confirming whether, for all experiments, they have reported all measures, conditions, data exclusions, and how they determined their sample sizes. The authors should, of course, add any additional text to ensure the statement is accurate.[6]

Preregistration is another process that is moving us toward more credible science. Preregistration is a process whereby researchers, before collecting or analyzing their data, submit predictions and a data analysis plan to one of the emerging online sites set up for this purpose. These preregistrations are digitally time-stamped when submitted, which allows clear identification of which analyses are testing predictions made in advance of the analysis and which are exploratory or developed later in the research process. The goal of preregistration is not to prevent exploratory analyses beyond the planned analyses but simply to make clear what was predicted in advance and what was not. Rather than viewing preregistration as preventing exploration, the Data Colada trio view it as informing readers of when the empirical work follows prespecified hypotheses and analytic plans.[7]

At the start of 2024, there were two primary platforms created by nonprofit organizations on which social scientists could preregister their work: http://AsPredicted.org and http://osf.io. The former allows researchers to complete a simple form by answering eight short questions about their research, while the latter allows a research team to coordinate its research collaboration with time-stamped documents that mark the actual order of progress on a research project. The use of these platforms has grown dramatically in recent years.

One interesting observation about the scandals discussed throughout this book is that the alleged frauds have not been very sophisticated. If the data had been publicly available, it would not have been difficult for a good data detective to see. Thus one quick step on the road to reform is for journals to require researchers to make their data publicly available—ideally by posting it online. If researchers were aware that the growing community of skeptics could review their data, the temptation to engage in fraudulent behavior likely would be reduced.

These new demands undoubtedly create costs to honest researchers. This is true of the steps that we take in broader society to reduce fraud. The need to fund the forensic professionals at the Internal Revenue Service would not be needed if all taxpayers were honest. But that state does not exist for taxpayers or for researchers, imposing the need to incur the cost on all of us.

There is also an issue of equity involved when we increase the costs of doing research. It is easier for researchers at well-funded institutions to absorb these costs. Researchers at less-well-funded institutions, already at a disadvantage, will have more hurdles to jump. I wish there were an easy solution to this possible inequity (e.g., a subsidy system created by journals or professional organizations), but that is unlikely to quickly emerge.

**Changing Co-author Expectations**

My 2022 book, *Complicit: How We Enable the Unethical and How to Stop*, covered many of the scandals you have read about or watched movies about in recent years.[8] But instead of focusing on Elizabeth Holmes, the Sackler family, or Harvey Weinstein, *Complicit* looked at those who surrounded such unethical actors and allowed their behavior to occur. In fact, as I write in the book, wrongdoers are almost always enabled by other people. Complicity comes in different forms. Some complicitors intentionally enable wrongdoers (explicit), while others enable them without realizing they are doing so (implicit). I believe that implicit complicity is most relevant to the challenges facing co-authors, who have no intent to allow unethical behavior to occur. But when co-authors trust those who act in fraudulent ways, their trust is a choice that can make them complicit even if they were not aware that fraud was occurring.

I have heard Uri Simonsohn say that academic fraud is rarely a collaborative effort. That is, across the many scandals he has followed, he is not aware of any evidence of collusion in the commission of research fraud. Yet if we think about who had the closest view of alleged fraud and the biggest hints it was taking place, it is likely to be the fraudster's co-authors. It is clear to me that I had hints about the signing-first paper that I did not fully pursue. As I documented, I was the co-author who asked the most questions about orange flags that emerged, but I didn't ask enough of them. In other cases of research fraud that I've studied, there were often early hints of wrongdoing that co-authors didn't pursue. The co-authors were not aware of the fraud, but that was in part because they didn't look for it—they were implicitly complicit. Maybe they didn't have incentives to look for possible fraud because they were benefiting from the success that the fraudulent co-author was providing. Maybe they had confidence in the wisdom of a famous co-author or deferred to the authority of a senior professor. And, most important, as was true for me, maybe they simply trusted their colleagues.[9]

My assessment is that the biggest reason co-authors become implicitly complicit in research fraud is trust. Trust leads us to rely on our co-authors' work without skepticism. It allows us to believe pretty unbelievable effects—for example, that moving a signature could lead to an average change in mileage reporting of over 2,000 miles. In retrospect, the magnitude of this effect should have been a hint of a problem, but trust remained a barrier. When I saw something even more unbelievable—that a group of tens of thousands of drivers were driving over 25,000 miles per year—I did ask questions. But when Mazar provided a viable explanation, my trust led me to accept a plausible answer (that the period between mileage reporting was more than a year). My trust kept me from exploring the data myself, and I benefited by trusting my co-authors. By trusting, a researcher has more time for other interesting projects or more time for nonwork activities. And, when we perceive time to be scarce, trust helps address the shortage of time.

I recommend that the open science movement enlist co-authors in the effort to create more credible science. Specifically, I believe researchers should make two commitments. First, we should all have a norm that when something seems off, we should investigate thoroughly until we arrive at a solid answer. I have often told a story about when I failed to explore and speak up about a hint of corruption that I observed during a consulting assignment for the U.S. government. Executives who hear the story are quick to let me off of the hook, noting that I didn't know that something was wrong. In contrast, journalists tend to agree with me that I should have investigated the issue more closely. They argue that the best stories are found by pursuing matters where the details don't add up and simple answers fail to resolve the ambiguity. For me, the message is that co-authors should pay attention to hints when the facts don't add up and investigate until they are confident that they have a good understanding of what happened.

Some people have questioned my lack of suspicion about Gino's productivity. I can only say that at the time of her peak productivity, I never considered the possibility of Gino or any of my very productive co-authors committing fraud. I can easily find fault in my unwavering trust in my co-authors, given what followed. Others have asked me whether I noticed Gino taking control of data collection on studies long after she had the doctoral students, support staff, and financial resources needed to assign this work to others. Quite honestly, I do not recall having any discussion with my co-authors about Gino managing the data collection for the lab studies in the signing-first project. For many years after the paper was published, I assumed that Shu had been actively involved in the data collection. I now feel a much stronger need to verify data in papers that will have my name on them.

Second, I think we should change our collaborations so at least one additional person reviews the data and the details of the analysis, beyond the core person collecting the data or doing the analytics. Honest researchers should be happy to have an extra set of eyes on their work. If authors could verify that their data had been reviewed by a second set of eyes, anyone reading it could view it as more reliable. Separate from ethical concerns, it has been well documented that many errors are made in the production of social science publications. A second set of eyes would have the additional benefit of eliminating such errors. Finally, any potential fraudster might be less likely to engage in data fabrication if they knew that someone else would be looking closely at the data. We are also witnessing creative new approaches to laboratory management. Multiple junior faculty members at HBS have created a document on ethical research practices to guide their labs. Our institutions should be demanding this kind of integrity and transparency—more on that below.

As I finish writing this book, Uri Simonsohn has let me know that Data Colada is creating a new platform called AsCollected that will allow co-authors to document details about their data collection and analysis, the identity of which co-author was involved in each aspect of the project, and information about where and when the data collection took place.

Such changes in co-author expectations and procedures can be implemented. The only significant shift would be from viewing questions as an indication of mistrust to viewing questions as simply part of the responsibility of being a co-author. Senior colleagues who run labs and have administrative responsibility have the power to change this norm in their institutions. We can do so by highlighting that these are changes that social science needs to recover its reputation, rather than changes that reflect a collapse of trust within research groups.

These thoughts on co-authorship responsibilities are aimed at the future; I do not blame researchers for not following these processes in the past. As was true of p-hacking before 2011, we simply were not aware that we needed to be vigilant on this front. But there is no justification for continuing our past mistakes. We need to move toward a norm where we do trust our co-authors, while understanding that when we check one another's work, we are doing our job in an open science environment.

**Journal Changes**

A lot has changed in the field of psychology since the 2011 p-hacking paper was published, and a lot continues to change. Thus it is hard to capture a static picture of the state of the revolution or renaissance in psychology. One way to take a snapshot of the direction of the field is to look at the changes being made at one prominent journal, *Psychological Science*. Some researchers believe that the journal's policy of publishing short articles contributed to the lack of disclosure in the field in the first decade of the millennium. Yet by 2014, editor Eric Eich had implemented stronger disclosure rules at *Psychological Science*. Eich also introduced several new initiatives to raise ethical standards, including removing word limits for Methods sections (which could have worked against full transparency) and introducing "badges" to encourage preregistration and sharing of data and materials. Authors of manuscripts accepted by *Psychological Science*[10] could earn up to three badges for participating in open science practices—specifically, for making their data publicly available, making their materials available, and preregistering their studies. Papers with badges can be seen as more credible to readers. By 2022, 69 percent of articles published in *Psychological Science* had an open data badge, 55 percent had an open materials badge, and 43 percent had a preregistration badge.[11]

These enhanced disclosure rules were extended by Eich's successor, Stephen Lindsey, who took over as editor in 2016. Meanwhile, open science activist Simine Vazire was creating new disclosure rules as editor of the journal *Social Psychological and Personality Science*.[12] Vazire's appointment as the new editor of *Psychological Science* in 2024 signaled that the field saw a need for increased data transparency. Vazire implemented a requirement that data, original research materials, and analysis scripts be made public in a trusted third-party repository. Realizing that there might be ethical, legal, and practical reasons for keeping some data out of the public eye, *Psychological Science*, under Vazire, specified processes the editorial team could follow to consider transparency exceptions on a case-by-case basis.[13] With its new transparency requirements, *Psychological Science* eliminated the open science badges, as many of the requirements for obtaining the badges were now mandatory for publication. While I am enthusiastic about Vazire's changes, it is important to understand that these changes will be more difficult for researchers at less-well-funded institutions.

Vazire also introduced "registered reports," which allowed authors to submit their work (predictions, methods, etc.) for peer review at *Psychological Science* and potentially be granted "in-principle acceptance" before they collected data. In-principle acceptance implies that the journal plans to accept the paper based on competent execution and presentation of the work. Registered reports were designed to reduce the opportunity for author bias to affect data collection and analysis—or to prevent "bias stemming from editors' decisions during peer review," as Vazire and Tom E. Hardwicke, a new senior editor at the journal, stated in an article outlining the new protocols.[14]

Vazire appointed Hardwicke as the leader of a new group of editors focused on statistics, transparency, and rigor (STAR). STAR editors will assist the journal's primary editors as needed on methodological issues. They will also perform light transparency checks on all manuscripts sent for peer review and more in-depth checks on manuscripts that pass peer review, receive "conditional acceptance," and are headed toward publication. STAR editors will also perform reproducibility checks on all accepted papers.

In addition, Vazire introduced a new partnership with the Institute for Replication (I4R, https://i4replication.org). I4R is a not-for-profit where researchers collaborate to verify the reproducibility, robustness, and replicability of published research articles. Starting in 2022, I4R focused on articles in leading economic and political science journals. The new partnership would add psychology. As of January 1, 2024, papers published in *Psychological Science* became candidates for post-publication verification audits by I4R. One additional change was to require authors to state in a Research Transparency Statement which aspects of each of their studies (research questions, hypotheses, design, and/or analyses) were preregistered and whether there had been any minor or major deviations from the original research plan.[15]

The changes that Vazire instituted were major for psychologists submitting their work to *Psychological Science*. Some of these changes will permanently change the research process. Others will themselves change or be eliminated over time. But they exemplify the field's desire to create, in Vazire and Hardwicke's words, "a more rigorous, verifiable, efficient, cumulative, and self-correcting science."[16]

Most psychology journals will move more slowly than *Psychological Science*. But change is inevitable, and it is the price we must pay to restore the field's credibility. Concerns and hesitancy about making broad changes can be seen in an editorial statement by the co-editors of *Organizational Behavior and Human Decision Processes*, Mike Baer and Maryam Kouchaki, who in February 2024 wrote:

> Over the last several years, OBHDP has taken important steps . . . such as requiring pre-registration for all new studies conducted during the review process, mandating clear reporting, and encouraging authors to make all study materials and data available to reviewers and readers. It is time to take the next step. Over the next months, we will be codifying the journal's position on each aspect of the research process . . . we want to assure authors that our policies will balance the need for integrity and transparency without being exclusionary. . . . A measured approach will ensure that the diverse research approaches we welcome are not excluded from submission.[17]

This statement reflects the demands and conflict that many social science journal editors are experiencing. I have noted similar small changes by other journals, including *Administrative Science Quarterly* and the *Journal of Consumer Research*. In my judgment, we will look back at Vazire as a hero and view others as adapting too slowly to our new reality.

**Universities Must Face Their Obligations**

As we've seen, reformers in the open science movement are outlining viable changes to the process of conducting social science. Many social scientists are implementing new processes in their research. And journals are starting to require key improvements to the scientific process for authors who seek to publish with them. Yet the universities that host and support social science research have been too slow to move toward promoting more credible social science. Researchers are using university resources, and those who use questionable research practices are putting their university's reputations on the line. It is time for universities to join the open science movement. This will help them safeguard their prestige and contribute to the integrity of the science they foster.

To begin, a university would be well served by creating a task force that would consider requiring some of the best practices outlined in this chapter and implemented by journals like *Psychological Science*. Rather than merely outsourcing the task of reforming social science, universities need to deliberate over how they think social science should be conducted in their institutions. I obviously have some strong opinions about the changes that universities should make, but I do not possess the answers. Researchers at universities should reflect and deliberate on the changes that are needed. They have the ability to identify changes that will enhance the integrity of research conducted at their institutions.

Universities should also consider the incentives they are providing for hiring and promotion. Are they rewarding scholars for quantity of publication rather than quality and for following ethical scientific practices? Many of the other steps I have outlined would also reduce the incentives of social scientists to engage in unethical behavior.

In the aftermath of data-fabrication stories, American universities have maintained enormous secrecy. Typically, a professor has resigned, and the university has provided very limited information about why. Across the U.S. stories profiled in this book, there has been little evidence that universities have investigated the broader set of publications by the resigning professor apart from the limited number of papers retracted. This leaves the professor's co-authors, the broader research community, and the public in the dark about the trustworthiness of work by the professor that has not been retracted. As I documented earlier, I was left in the dark, unable to provide good answers to colleagues who asked me whether Harvard was burying the Gino story. Two years was a long time to wait. Yet the anonymous junior colleagues in the Hauser story waited three years for Harvard to act (and five years for the federal government to act) while they pursued their early careers as doctoral students, postdocs, and junior faculty members at other universities.

In both the Hauser and Gino stories, university officials allowed these scholars under investigation to continue their work and publish their new research as the university investigated. Many parties affected would argue that too little attention was given to protecting the large number of junior colleagues affected during these investigations. In such cases, the few colleagues who know about a possible investigation are left in the lurch when asked by students whether they should work in the lab of a faculty member under likely investigation. The longer the investigation, the larger the problems that are created for the colleagues involved.

The time taken in the Gino and Hauser investigations contrasts sharply with the investigation of Diederik Stapel by Tilburg University (as well as by the University of Groningen and the University of Amsterdam). I am not a lawyer, and I assume that the laws of a university's host country can significantly affect its action. And I assume that my university was thoughtful about its legal obligation. Yet I worry that the concerns of universities for due process for the scholar under investigation and for the university's legal liability may come at the expense of the welfare of junior scholars and maintaining academic credibility.

Finally, and relatedly, universities need to give more support to the coauthors of fraudsters, particularly junior researchers, in the aftermath of data-fabrication scandals. One compelling perspective on this issue comes from Marret K. Noordewier, now on the faculty of the psychology department of Leiden University, the Netherlands. As noted in chapter 9, Stapel had been Noordewier's PhD and postdoctoral adviser when his frauds were uncovered in 2011. Though the evidence overwhelmingly implicated Stapel as a lone fraudster, he fabricated data for publications that had numerous co-authors, including Noordewier. Stapel's co-authors were left to deal with the consequences of his actions.[18]

As I shared in chapter 9, Noordewier described, in a 2023 article, how the Stapel scandal left her facing years of wasted work, retracted papers, unwanted media attention, and suspicious prosecutors.[19] Hoping to reboot her career, she pursued a second PhD, but came to terms with the fact that the scandal would always follow her. Noordewier offers advice to universities in the aftermath of data fabrication stories:

> Ask the involved researchers what they need. No one can be prepared for the consequences of being affected by scientific misconduct. . . . Those affected may need legal help, advice on how to deal with the media and psychological help with picking up the pieces. . . . If we do not want researchers to be slowed down

beyond the time they have already lost, there needs to be room for nonstandard decisions in (for example) grant applications, hiring decisions and promotion criteria. Recognize what people have accomplished and appreciate the work that is still valid, meaningful and useful.

Make sure researchers feel safe and free to share their concerns and needs. Responsible research practices are not only about research, but also about researchers and the culture we work in. This includes the support of those who are affected by scientific misconduct.

Noordewier's insights could help universities develop better responses in the aftermath of research fraud. In contrast, to date, the American experience has been one of silence. As Brian Nosek has noted, it's uncommon for U.S.-based institutions to make their investigations public.

This closing chapter has focused on the role of researchers, lab leaders, journals, and universities. Funding agencies and the government should also be interested in how their resources are spent, and should consider implementing many of the ideas that have been outlined. This would lead to more funded research being replicable by others.

**Silence**

Overlapping with Data Colada's 2021 and 2023 publications regarding the 2012 signing-first paper, I became involved with Fellowships at Auschwitz for the Study of Professional Ethics (FASPE). FASPE is a not-for-profit organization created in response to two societal forces. One was the view of the founder, David Goldman, that there has been a breakdown in the ethics of the most important professions in contemporary society. Second, there were parallels to the failure of professionals in Germany and Poland in the years leading up to and during the Holocaust. According to its web page:

> Each year, FASPE awards 80 to 90 Fellowships to graduate students and early-career professionals in Business, Seminary, Design & Technology, Journalism, Law, and Medicine. The Fellowships begin with intense study in Germany and Poland where FASPE takes advantage of the urgency created by the power of place to translate the history into the present.[20]

Based on the publication of my 2022 book, *Complicit*, FASPE invited me to be a keynote speaker at its 2023 alumni conference. I was then invited to be one of the faculty members on the May–June 2024 trip to Berlin, Krakow, and Auschwitz with the Business, Law, and Design & Technology fellows. While writing this book, I was also catching up on my knowledge of Nazi Germany by reading lots of papers and books and watching movies. A core part of what I learned, which is strongly highlighted by the FASPE staff, is the enormous role that silence played in allowing the Nazis to rise to power, which led to the demise of between 70 and 85 million people.[21] The harms created by the Nazi regime between 1933 and 1945 could not have happened without the silence of many.

Silence is easy to understand. Many of those silent in Germany between 1933 and 1945 would have been risking their lives by speaking up. Others were not at risk and simply stayed quiet, as they did not see their involvement to be part of their role in society. In the stories documented in this book, many were complicit through inaction rather than through actions. When we fail to speak up to create value, or when we facilitate evil by viewing wrongdoing as not our concern, we may well be complicit.

Beyond thinking about our own potential to prevent harm, we should also think about the role of institutional leaders in creating a culture that rewards individuals for speaking up. As I spoke to the whistleblowers in some of the stories in this book, I was struck by the failure of university leaders to give adequate consideration to the risks the whistleblowers were taking for the collective good. The whistleblowers had to act against the informal pressures of their institution. Our leaders can do better.

There are lots of reasons to remain silent—"It's not my job," "The institution discouraged me from leaking information," "I don't want to harm my friends," "I could be punished for speaking up." But when too many remain silent, evil is more likely to occur. This leads me to have additional admiration for those who rise to the challenge and simply do the right thing. My admiration for those who have spoken up in the past was a significant motivation for writing this book.

I would be naïve to think that I alone have the answers on how researchers, co-authors, journals, and universities should respond to the current crisis in confidence within social science research. The suggestions in this chapter are simply my best attempt to organize some of the ideas that have emerged. Others have had and will have wiser ideas. But to restore the credibility of social science, we need to engage with these challenges more strongly—something we have been slow to do so far.

# Gratitude

In this book, you have read about colleagues of mine who helped me understand the core story I've recounted. Many close friends have listened patiently as I described my experience on the signing-first paper. Many of my co-authors have shared their experiences with me, often at considerable emotional cost. Others have questioned the wisdom of writing this account. All of them have helped me better understand the worst chapter in my academic career. I truly appreciate their generosity and friendship. These individuals have also helped me formulate the recommendations in chapter 12 on how to move the field of psychology forward with impact and integrity.

I conducted dozens of interviews to better understand this story. Most interviewees decided, whether before or after the interview, to remain anonymous. I honor their request and want them to know that I very much appreciate the information and insights they provided. Others who have shared their experiences with me include Ellen Evers, Yoel Inbar, Julia Minson, Don Moore, Brian Nosek, Todd Rogers, Michael Sanders, Uri Simonsohn, Scott Wiltermuth, and Marcel Zeelenberg.

I received feedback on earlier drafts of this project from Jon Abbott, Jonathan Albano, Dolly Chugh, Sara Dadkhah, Marla Felcher, David Luban, Kathleen McGinn, Katy Milkman, Don Moore, Julia Minson, Brian Nosek, Todd Rogers, Nika Rudenko, and many others who chose to remain anonymous. The book is more comprehensive and clearer thanks to their wise and informative input.

I also benefited from the insightful contributions of Catherine Woods, my editor at the MIT Press. My presentation of the story was improved enormously by the editorial help of Katie Shonk. I appreciate Elizabeth Sweeny's careful and precise proofreading, error-checking, and reference correcting. I hope that all who read this account, including those who helped me tell this story, find the final version to be a useful contribution to social science.

With gratitude,

Max H. Bazerman

# Notes

**Preface**

1. L. Shu, N. Mazar, F. Gino, D. Ariely, and M. Bazerman, "Signing at the Beginning Makes Ethics Salient and Decreases Dishonest Self-Reports in Comparison to Signing at the End," *Proceedings of the National Academy of Sciences* 109, no. 38 (2012): 15197–15200.

2. A. S. Kristal, A. V. Whillans, M. H. Bazerman, F. Gino, L. L. Shu, N. Mazar, and D. Ariely, "Signing at the Beginning versus at the End Does Not Decrease Dishonesty," *Proceedings of the National Academy of Sciences* 117, no. 13 (2020): 7103–7107.

3. http://datacolada.org.

4. Max H. Bazerman, *Complicit: How We Enable the Unethical and How to Stop* (Princeton University Press, 2022).

**Chapter 1**

1. L. Shu, N. Mazar, F. Gino, D. Ariely, and M. Bazerman, "Signing at the Beginning Makes Ethics Salient and Decreases Dishonest Self-Reports in Comparison to Signing at the End, *Proceedings of the National Academy of Sciences* 109, no. 38 (2012): 15197–15200.

2. http://datacolada.org.

3. U. Simonsohn, J. Simmons, and L. Nelson, "Evidence of Fraud in an Influential Field Experiment About Dishonesty," Data Colada, August 17, 2021. http://datacolada.org/98.

4. https://www.science.org/content/article/after-honesty-researcher-s-retractions-colleagues-expand-scrutiny-her-work.

5. https://www.washingtonpost.com/archive/politics/2005/06/20/expert-says-he-was-told-to-soften-tobacco-testimony/6bef641b-caad-42d4-9987-719c000c0976.

6. https://en.wikipedia.org/wiki/Robert_McCallum_Jr.

7. https://www.newyorker.com/magazine/2023/10/09/they-studied-dishonesty-was-their-work-a-lie.

**Chapter 2**

1. R. C. Mayer, J. H. Davis, and F. D. Schoorman, "An Integrative Model of Organizational Trust," *Academy of Management Review* 20, no. 3 (1995): 709–734.

2. F. Gino and M. H. Bazerman, "When Misconduct Goes Unnoticed: The Acceptability of Gradual Erosion in Others' Unethical Behavior," *Journal of Experimental Social Psychology* 45, no. 4 (2009): 708–719.

3. L. Shu, F. Gino, and M. H. Bazerman, "Dishonest Deed, Clear Conscience: When Cheating Leads to Moral Disengagement and Motivated Forgetting," *Personality and Social Psychology Bulletin* 37, no. 3 (2011): 330–349.

4. https://www.youtube.com/watch?v=CjgGUzEmQYk.

5. Thomas T. Hoopes Prize, Harvard College, 2006; Seymour E. and Ruth B. Harris Prize, Department of Economics, Harvard University, 2006; Faculty Prize, Department of Psychology, Harvard University, 2006.

6. https://www.nytimes.com/2015/10/11/fashion/weddings/lisa-shu-matthew-wilson.html.

7. "Behavioral Researcher Says He 'Undoubtedly Made a Mistake' in False Data Scandal," *The Times of Israel*, September 4, 2021.

8. "The 'Irrational' Way Humans Interact with Dentists," NPR.org, October 5, 2010. Retrieved January 28, 2022.

9. "Letters: Dentists," NPR.org, October 13, 2010. Retrieved January 28, 2022.

10. Dan Ariely, *The (Honest) Truth About Dishonesty: How We Lie to Everyone—Especially Ourselves* (Harper Perennial, 2012).

11. On Amir, Dan Ariely, and Nina Mazar, "The Dishonesty of Honest People: A Theory of Self-Concept Maintenance," *Journal of Marketing Research* 45 (2008): 633–634.

12. https://www.chronicle.com/article/is-dan-ariely-telling-the-truth.

13. https://www.newyorker.com/magazine/2023/10/09/they-studied-dishonesty-was-their-work-a-lie.

14. https://twitter.com/R_Thaler/status/1678993443027312641

15. https://www.chronicle.com/article/is-dan-ariely-telling-the-truth.

16. https://www.chronicle.com/article/is-dan-ariely-telling-the-truth.

17. https://ninamazar.com.

18. https://ninamazar.com.

19. Max H. Bazerman, *Complicit: How We Enable the Unethical and How to Stop* (Princeton University Press, 2022).

## Chapter 3

1. L. T. Benjamin, "America, History of Popular Psychology," in *Encyclopedia of the History of Psychological Theories*, ed. R. W. Rieber (Springer, 2012).

2. Benjamin, "America, History of Popular Psychology."

3. Benjamin, "America, History of Popular Psychology."

4. Barbara Spellman, "A Short (Personal) Future History of Revolution 2.0," *Perspectives on Psychological Science* 10 (2015): 886–899.

5. https://bookauthority.org/books/best-selling-psychology-books.

6. D. J. Bem, "Feeling the Future: Experimental Evidence for Anomalous Retroactive Influences on Cognition and Affect," *Journal of Personality and Social Psychology* 100, no. 3 (2011): 407–425.

7. Leif D. Nelson, Joseph P. Simmons, and Uri Simonsohn, "Psychology's Renaissance," *Annual Review of Psychology* 69 (2018): 511–534.

8. Etienne P. LeBel, and Kurt R. Peters, "Fearing the Future of Empirical Psychology: Bem's (2011) Evidence of Psi as a Case Study of Deficiencies in Modal Research Practice," *Review of General Psychology* 15, no. 4 (2011): 371–379.

9. J. Galak, R. A. LeBoeuf, L. D. Nelson, and J. P. Simmons, "Correcting the Past: Failures to Replicate Psi," *Journal of Personality and Social Psychology* 103, no. 6 (2012): 933–948.

10. Z. Kekecs, B. Palfi, B. Szaszi, et al., "Raising the Value of Research Studies in Psychological Science by Increasing the Credibility of Research Reports: The Transparent Psi Project," 2023 *Royal Society Open Science* (February 2023).

11. Daniel Engber, "Daryl Bem Proved ESP Is Real: Which Means Science Is Broken," *Slate*, May 17, 2017.

12. Engber, "Daryl Bem Proved ESP Is Real."

13. https://www.newyorker.com/magazine/2023/10/09/they-studied-dishonesty-was-their-work-a-lie.

14. Joseph P. Simmons, Leif D. Nelson, and Uri Simonsohn, "False-Positive Psychology: Undisclosed Flexibility in Data Collection and Analysis Allows Presenting Anything as Significant," *Psychological Science* 22 (November 2011): 1359–1366.

15. DataColada.org.

16. "Scientific Method," Wikipedia.

17. L. K. John, G. Loewenstein, and D. Prelec, "Measuring the Prevalence of Questionable Research Practices with Incentives for Truth Telling," *Psychological Science* 23, no. 5 (2012): 524–532.

18. S. Doyen, O. Klein, C. L. Pichon, and A. Cleeremans, "Behavioral Priming: It's All in the Mind, but Whose Mind?," *PLOS ONE* 7, no. 1 (2012): e29081.

19. J. A. Bargh, M. Chen, and L. Burrows, "Automaticity of Social Behavior: Direct Effects of Trait Construct and Stereotype-Activation on Action," *Journal of Personality and Social Psychology* 71 (1996): 230–244.

20. https://www.nationalgeographic.com/science/article/failed-replication-bargh-psychology-study-doyen.

21. Doyen, Klein, Pichon, and Cleeremans, "Behavioral Priming."

22. https://www.nationalgeographic.com/science/article/failed-replication-bargh-psychology-study-doyen.

23. https://www.nationalgeographic.com/science/article/failed-replication-bargh-psychology-study-doyen.

24. https://www.nature.com/news/polopoly_fs/7.6716.1349271308!/suppinfoFile/Kahneman%20Letter.pdf.

25. https://www.nature.com/articles/nature.2012.11535

26. D. R. Carney, A. J. C. Cuddy, and A. Yap, "Power Posing: Brief Nonverbal Displays Affect Neuroendocrine Levels and Risk Tolerance," *Psychological Science* 21, no. 10 (2010): 1363–1368.

27. https://www.ted.com/talks/amy_cuddy_your_body_language_may_shape_who_you_are?language=en.

28. A. J. C. Cuddy, *Presence: Bringing Your Boldest Self to Your Biggest Challenges* (Little, Brown, 2015).

29. E. Ranehill, A. Dreber, M. Johannesson, S. Leiberg, S. Sul, and R. A. Weber, "Assessing the Robustness of Power Posing: No Effect on Hormones and Risk Tolerance in a Large Sample of Men and Women," *Psychological Science* 26, no. 5 (2015): 653–656.

30. D. R. Carney, A. J. C. Cuddy, and A. Yap, "Review and Summary of Research on the Embodied Effects of Expansive (vs. Contractive) Nonverbal Displays," *Psychological Science* 26, no. 5 (2015): 657–663.

# Notes

31. https://datacolada.org/37.

32. https://faculty.haas.berkeley.edu/dana_carney/pdf_My%20position%20on%20power%20poses.pdf.

33. A. J. C. Cuddy, S. J. Schultz, and N. E. Fosse, "P-Curving a More Comprehensive Body of Research on Postural Feedback Reveals Clear Evidential Value for Power-Posing Effects: Reply to Simmons and Simonsohn (2017)," *Psychological Science* 29, no. 4 (2018): 656–666.

34. https://guides.uflib.ufl.edu/c.php?g=147659&p=967536.

35. Leif D. Nelson, Joseph P. Simmons, and Uri Simonsohn, "Psychology's Renaissance," *Annual Review of Psychology* 69 (2018): 511–534.

36. Open Science Collaboration, "Estimating the Reproducibility of Psychological Science," *Science* 349 (2015): Article aac4716.

37. Open Science Collaboration, "Estimating the Reproducibility of Psychological Science."

38. Daniel Gilbert, Gary King, Stephen Pettigrew, and Timothy Wilson, "Replication Data for: Comment on 'Estimating the Reproducibility of Psychological Science,'" *Science* 35 (2016): 1037–1038.

39. Gilbert, King, Pettigrew, and Wilson, "Replication Data for: Comment on 'Estimating the Reproducibility.'"

40. Nelson, Simmons, and Simonsohn, "Psychology's Renaissance."

41. https://www.newyorker.com/magazine/2023/10/09/they-studied-dishonesty-was-their-work-a-lie.

42. https://twitter.com/DanTGilbert/status/470199929626193921.

43. Stephanie M. Lee, "Scholar Accused of Research Fraud Sues Harvard and Data Sleuths, Alleging a 'Smear Campaign,'" *The Chronicle of Higher Education*, August 2, 2023, https://www.chronicle.com/article/scholar-accused-of-research-fraud-sues-harvard-and-data-sleuths-alleging-a-smear-campaign.

44. https://www.newyorker.com/magazine/2023/10/09/they-studied-dishonesty-was-their-work-a-lie.

45. https://twitter.com/siminevazire/status/1686913939962216448.

46. Wolfgang Stroebe, Tom Postmes, and Russell Spears, "Scientific Misconduct and the Myth of Self-Correction in Science," *Perspectives in Psychological Science* 7, no. 6 (2012): 670–688.

47. Barbara Spellman, "A Short (Personal) Future History of Revolution 2.0," *Perspectives in Psychological Science* 10 (2015): 866–899.

48. Spellman, "A Short (Personal) Future History of Revolution 2.0."

49. https://freakonomics.com/podcast/can-academic-fraud-be-stopped.

50. S. Vazire, "The Next Chapter for Psychological Science," *Psychological Science* 35, no. 7 (2023), https://doi.org/10.1177/09567976231221558.

## Chapter 4

1. Google Scholar, https://scholar.google.com/citations?view_op=view_citation&hl=en&user=NGKWT4gAAAAJ&cstart=20&pagesize=80&citation_for_view=NGKWT4gAAAAJ:3htObqc8RwsC.

2. https://obamawhitehouse.archives.gov/sites/default/files/microsites/ostp/sbst_2015_annual_report_final_9_14_15.pdf.

3. Richard H. Thaler and Cass R. Sunstein, *Nudge: Improving Decisions About Health, Wealth, and Happiness* (Yale University Press, 2008).

4. Michael Luca and Max H. Bazerman, *The Power of Experiments: Decision Making in a Data-Driven World* (MIT Press, 2022).

5. https://www.npr.org/transcripts/1190568472.

6. Stewart Kettle, Marco Hernandez, Michael Sanders, Oliver Hauser, and Simon Ruda, "Failure to CAPTCHA Attention: Null Results from an Honesty Priming Experiment in Guatemala," *Behavioral Sciences* 7, no. 2 (2017): 28.

7. https://www.fastcompany.com/3068506/lemonade-is-using-behavioral-science-to-onboard-customers-and-keep-them-honest.

8. https://www.hbs.edu/faculty/Pages/item.aspx?num=59687.

9. A. S. Kristal, A. V. Whillans, M. H. Bazerman, F. Gino, L. L. Shu, N. Mazar, and D. Ariely, "Signing at the Beginning versus at the End Does Not Decrease Dishonesty," *Proceedings of the National Academy of Sciences* 117, no. 13 (2020): 7103–7107.

10. Max H. Bazerman, *Complicit: How We Enable the Unethical and How to Stop* (Princeton University Press, 2022).

## Chapter 5

1. https://www.newyorker.com/magazine/2023/10/09/they-studied-dishonesty-was-their-work-a-lie.

2. Chen-Bo Zhong and Katie Liljenquist, "Washing Away Your Sins: Threatened Morality and Physical Cleansing," *Science* 313, no. 5792 (2006): 1451–1452.

# Notes

3. Jennifer V. Fayard, Amandeep K. Bassi, Daniel M. Bernstein, and Brent W. Roberts, "Is Cleanliness Next to Godliness? Dispelling Old Wives' Tales: Failure to Replicate Zhong and Liljenquist (2006)," *Journal of Articles in Support of the Null Hypothesis* 6, no. 2 (2009): 21–30; Brian D. Earp, Jim A. C. Everett, Elizabeth N. Madva, and J. Kiley Hamlin, "Out, Damned Spot: Can the 'Macbeth Effect' Be Replicated?," *Basic and Applied Social Psychology* 36 (2014): 91–98.

4. https://www.theorgplumber.com/posts/statement.

5. https://www.theorgplumber.com/posts/statement.

6. https://www.theorgplumber.com/posts/statement.

7. https://www.newyorker.com/magazine/2023/10/09/they-studied-dishonesty-was-their-work-a-lie.

8. https://journals.aom.org/doi/abs/10.5465/AMBPP.2022.15161abstract.

9. https://www.newyorker.com/magazine/2023/10/09/they-studied-dishonesty-was-their-work-a-lie.

10. Stephanie M. Lee, "A Famous Honesty Researcher Is Retracting a Study over Fake Data," BuzzFeed, August 20, 2021. Retrieved from https://www.buzzfeednews.com/article/stephaniemlee/dan-ariely-honesty-study-retraction.

11. Lee, "A Famous Honesty Researcher Is Retracting a Study."

12. Lee, "A Famous Honesty Researcher Is Retracting a Study."

13. https://openmkt.org/blog/2022/dan-ariely-claims-authorship-order-shields-him-from-blame-speculates-that-a-low-level-envelope-stuffer-committed-the-fraud.

14. http://datacolada.org/98.

15. https://datacolada.org/98.

16. The second 2020 paper was an adaptation of the main 2020 *PNAS* paper and published as Ariella Kristal, Ashley Whillans, Max Bazerman, Francesca Gino, Lisa Shu, Nina Mazar, and Dan Ariely, "When We're Wrong, It's Our Responsibility as Scientists to Say So," *Scientific American*, March 21, 2020.

## Chapter 6

1. https://www.chronicle.com/article/a-weird-research-misconduct-scandal-about-dishonesty-just-got-weirder.

2. https://poetsandquants.com/2023/09/01/these-b-school-professors-have-raised-more-than-300k-to-defend-themselves-from-francesca-ginos-lawsuit.

3. https://datacolada.org.

4. https://datacolada.org.

5. https://poetsandquants.com/2023/08/04/what-francesca-ginos-harvard-lawsuit-says-about-data-coladas-fraud-allegations/?pq-category=business-school-news&pq-category-2=mba.

6. https://steamtraen.blogspot.com/2023/07/strange-numbers-in-dataset-of-zhang.html.

7. T. Zhang, F. Gino, and M. I. Norton, "The Surprising Effectiveness of Hostile Mediators," *Management Science* 63, no. 6 (2016): 1972–1992.

8. https://www.npr.org/2023/07/27/1190568472/dan-ariely-francesca-gino-harvard-dishonesty-fabricated-data.

9. https://www.chronicle.com/article/is-dan-ariely-telling-the-truth.

10. https://www.chronicle.com/article/is-dan-ariely-telling-the-truth.

11. https://www.npr.org/2023/07/27/1190568472/dan-ariely-francesca-gino-harvard-dishonesty-fabricated-data.

12. "Dan Ariely on Behavioral Economics," *Armchair Expert with Dax Shepard*, November 2, 2023, https://armchairexpertpod.com/pods/dan-ariely.

13. https://www.chronicle.com/article/duke-to-pay-112-5-million-to-settle-scientific-misconduct-lawsuit/.

14. https://www.chronicle.com/article/is-dan-ariely-telling-the-truth.

15. https://www.chronicle.com/article/is-dan-ariely-telling-the-truth.

16. https://academiccouncil.duke.edu/february-15-2024/.

17. https://www.chronicle.com/article/is-dan-ariely-telling-the-truth.

## Chapter 7

1. https://poetsandquants.com/2023/08/04/what-francesca-ginos-harvard-lawsuit-says-about-data-coladas-fraud-allegations/?pq-category=business-school-news&pq-category-2=mba.

2. https://www.nytimes.com/2023/09/30/business/the-harvard-professor-and-the-bloggers.html.

3. https://poetsandquants.com/2023/08/04/what-francesca-ginos-harvard-lawsuit-says-about-data-coladas-fraud-allegations/?pq-category=business-school-news&pq-category-2=mba.

# Notes

4. https://lessig.medium.com/on-francesca-gino-a4f88b4561e3.

5. https://storage.courtlistener.com/recap/gov.uscourts.mad.259933/gov.uscourts.mad.259933.19.0.pdf.

6. https://www.francesca-v-harvard.org/data-colada-post-1.

7. https://www.nytimes.com/2023/09/30/business/the-harvard-professor-and-the-bloggers.html.

8. https://www.newyorker.com/magazine/2023/10/09/they-studied-dishonesty-was-their-work-a-lie.

9. https://en.wikipedia.org/wiki/Francesca_Gino.

10. https://www.thecrimson.com/article/2023/10/18/hbs-faculty-speak-out/.

11. https://www.thecrimson.com/article/2024/3/19/gino-suggests-mazar-manipulation.

12. Kathleen O'Grady, "Embattled Harvard Honesty Professor Accused of Plagiarism," *Science*, April 9, 2024, https://www.science.org/content/article/embattled-harvard-honesty-professor-accused-plagiarism.

13. Leif Nelson, Joe Simmons, and Uri Simonsohn, "Our (First?) Day in Court," May 8, 2024, Data Colada, https://datacolada.org/116.

14. Nelson, Simmons, and Simonsohn, "Our (First?) Day in Court."

15. https://www.thecrimson.com/article/2024/9/12/judge-dismisses-gino-lawsuit-defamation-charges/.

## Chapter 8

1. https://www.apa.org/monitor/2010/07-08/misconduct.

2. https://www.federalregister.gov/documents/2008/07/22/E8-16741/findings-of-scientific-misconduct; https://grants.nih.gov/grants/guide/notice-files/NOT-OD-08-097.html.

3. https://www.jennifervonk.com/uploads/7/7/3/2/7732985/smeesterscase.pdf.

4. Ed Yong, "Q&A: Uri Simonsohn: The Data Detective," *Nature* 487, no. 7405 (July 5, 2012): 18–19.

5. https://www.jennifervonk.com/uploads/7/7/3/2/7732985/smeesterscase.pdf.

6. https://www.jennifervonk.com/uploads/7/7/3/2/7732985/smeesterscase.pdf.

7. https://www.jennifervonk.com/uploads/7/7/3/2/7732985/smeesterscase.pdf.

8. https://www.nature.com/articles/nature.2012.10968.

9. https://www.chronicle.com/article/harvard-finds-psychology-researcher-solely-responsible-for-scientific-misconduct/?sra=true&cid=gen_sign_in.

10. https://www.chronicle.com/article/harvard-finds-psychology-researcher-solely-responsible-for-scientific-misconduct/?sra=true&cid=gen_sign_in.

11. https://www.chronicle.com/article/harvard-finds-psychology-researcher-solely-responsible-for-scientific-misconduct/?sra=true&cid=gen_sign_in.

12. https://www.thecrimson.com/article/2010/8/14/hauser-probe-transparency-harvard.

13. https://www.chronicle.com/article/harvard-finds-psychology-researcher-solely-responsible-for-scientific-misconduct/?sra=true&cid=gen_sign_in.

14. Marc D. Hauser, *Moral Minds: The Nature of Right and Wrong* (Ecco/HarperCollins Publishers, 2006).

15. https://www.thenation.com/article/archive/disgrace-marc-hauser; https://marcdhauser.com/news-contexts/evilicious-cruelty-desire-denial.

16. Brett Dahlberg, "Cornell Food Researcher's Downfall Raises Larger Questions for Science," NPR, September 26, 2018, https://www.npr.org/sections/thesalt/2018/09/26/651849441/cornell-food-researchers-downfall-raises-larger-questions-for-science.

17. Dahlberg, "Cornell Food Researcher's Downfall Raises Larger Questions."

18. https://www.buzzfeednews.com/article/stephaniemlee/brian-wansink-cornell-p-hacking.

19. https://www.buzzfeednews.com/article/stephaniemlee/brian-wansink-cornell-p-hacking.

20. https://www.buzzfeednews.com/article/stephaniemlee/brian-wansink-cornell-p-hacking.

21. https://mindmatters.ai/2020/12/torturing-data-can-destroy-a-career-the-case-of-brian-wansink.

22. https://en.wikipedia.org/wiki/Brian_Wansink.

23. https://www.nytimes.com/2013/04/28/magazine/diederik-stapels-audacious-academic-fraud.html.

24. Wolfgang Stroebe, Tom Postmes, and Russell Spears, "Scientific Misconduct and the Myth of Self-Correction in Science," *Perspectives in Psychological Science* 7, no. 6 (2012): 670–688.

25. Interviews with Evers (January 21, 2023) and Inbar (January 27, 2023).

# Notes

26. Interview with Evers (January 21, 2023).

27. https://www.nytimes.com/2013/04/28/magazine/diederik-stapels-audacious-academic-fraud.html.

28. Interviews with Evers (January 21, 2023) and Inbar (January 27, 2023).

29. Yudhijit Bhattacharjee, "The Mind of a Con Man," *New York Times Magazine*, April 28, 2013, https://www.nytimes.com/2013/04/28/magazine/diederik-stapels-audacious-academic-fraud.html.

30. Bhattacharjee, "The Mind of a Con Man."

31. Bhattacharjee, "The Mind of a Con Man."

32. https://www.tilburguniversity.edu/sites/default/files/download/Final%20report%20Flawed%20Science_2.pdf.

33. https://www.tilburguniversity.edu/sites/default/files/download/Final%20report%20Flawed%20Science_2.pdf.

34. Yudhijith Bhattacharjee, "Stapel Gets Community Service for Fabricating Studies," *Science Insider*, June 28, 2013.

35. "Stapel betuigt openlijk 'diepe spijt'". Brabants Dagblad. 31 October 2011, translated at http://en.wikipedia.org/wiki/Diederik_Stapel#cite_note-26.

36. https://dennyborsboomcom.files.wordpress.com/2017/11/borsboomwagenmakers2013.pdf.

37. https://www.nature.com/articles/nature.2012.10968.

## Chapter 9

1. https://www.theamericanconservative.com/making-it-up-in-america.

2. https://www.science.org/content/article/final-report-stapel-affair-points-bigger-problems-social-psychology.

3. https://www.tilburguniversity.edu/sites/default/files/download/Final%20report%20Flawed%20Science_2.pdf.

4. https://www.listennotes.com/podcasts/two-psychologists/episode-4-the-replication-5IpUtzJk_HB/#google_vignette.

5. M. K. Noordewier, "Support for Those Affected by Scientific Misconduct Is Crucial," *Nature Human Behavior* 7, no. 6 (2023): 830.

6. Noordewier, "Support for Those Affected by Scientific Misconduct Is Crucial."

7. Noordewier, "Support for Those Affected by Scientific Misconduct Is Crucial."

8. https://datacolada.org/114.

9. Max H. Bazerman, *Negotiation: The Game Has Changed* (Princeton University Press, 2025).

**Chapter 10**

1. https://www.gofundme.com/f/uhbka-support-data-coladas-legal-defense.

2. I do not mean to overclaim credit here. I give most of the credit for this effort to Vazire, Flake, and Inbar. I use the word "we" simply to convey that I agreed to be a co-sponsor.

3. https://www.science.org/content/article/how-reform-minded-new-editor-psychology-s-flagship-journal-will-shake-things.

4. https://datacolada.org/113.

5. https://www.science.org/content/article/after-honesty-researcher-s-retractions-colleagues-expand-scrutiny-her-work.

6. Lee McIntyre, *How to Talk to a Science Denier: Conversations with Flat Earthers, Climate Deniers, and Others Who Defy Reason* (MIT Press, 2022).

7. https://www.nytimes.com/2023/11/30/opinion/human-behavior-nudge.html.

8. https://www.nytimes.com/2023/11/30/opinion/human-behavior-nudge.html.

**Chapter 11**

1. https://www.espn.com/nfl/news/story?id=3378990.

2. Gary S. Becker, "Crime and Punishment: An Economic Approach," *Journal of Political Economy* 76 (1968): 169–217.

3. Lawrence Kohlberg, *Essays on Moral Development, Vol 1. I: The Philosophy of Moral Development* (Harper & Row, 1981).

4. https://errorstatistics.files.wordpress.com/2014/12/fakingscience-20141214.pdf. This citation and all subsequent citations of *Ontsporing* refer to Nick Brown's translation of Stapel's Dutch manuscript.

5. https://errorstatistics.files.wordpress.com/2014/12/fakingscience-20141214.pdf.

6. *Ontsporing*, pp. 101–102.

7. *Ontsporing*, p. 167.

8. *Ontsporing*, p. 117.

9. *Ontsporing*, p. 226.

10. *Ontsporing,* p. 131.

11. *Ontsporing,* p. 121.

12. https://www.psychologicalscience.org/observer/derailed-the-rise-and-fall-of-diederik-stapel.

13. *Ontsporing,* p. 164.

14. https://www.nytimes.com/2013/04/28/magazine/diederik-stapels-audacious-academic-fraud.html.

15. https://www.nytimes.com/2013/04/28/magazine/diederik-stapels-audacious-academic-fraud.html.

16. https://www.tilburguniversity.edu/sites/default/files/download/Final%20report%20Flawed%20Science_2.pdf.

17. Marc D. Hauser, *Moral Minds: How Nature Designed Our Universal Sense of Right and Wrong* (Ecco/HarperCollins Publishers, 2006).

18. https://schwitzsplinters.blogspot.com/search?q=Gino.

19. https://schwitzsplinters.blogspot.com/search?q=Gino.

20. B. Tuckfield, "Making It (Up) in America," *The American Conservative,* September 13, 2023, https://www.theamericanconservative.com/making-it-up-in-america.

21. https://paddockpost.com/2022/09/28/executive-compensation-at-harvard-2.

22. https://www.hbs.edu/faculty/Pages/item.aspx?num=53562.

23. Dan Ariely, *The (Honest) Truth About Dishonesty: How We Lie to Everyone—Especially Ourselves* (Harper Perennial, 2012), 184.

24. F. Gino and D. Ariely, "The Dark Side of Creativity: Original Thinkers Can Be More Dishonest," *Journal of Personality and Social Psychology* 102, no. 3 (2012): 445–459.

25. Scott S. Wiltermuth, Lynne C. Vincent, and F. Gino, "Creativity in Unethical Behavior Attenuates Condemnation and Breeds Social Contagion: When Transgressions Seem to Create Little Harm," *Organizational Behavior and Human Decision Processes* 139 (March 2017).

26. Jackson G. Lu, Jordi Quoidbach, Francesca Gino, Alek Chakroff, William W. Maddux, and Adam D. Galinsky, "The Dark Side of Going Abroad: How Broad Foreign Experiences Increase Immoral Behavior," *Journal of Personality and Social Psychology* 112, no. 1 (January 2017): 1–16.

27. Celia Chui, Maryam Kouchaki, and Francesca Gino, "'Many Others Are Doing It, so Why Shouldn't I?' How Being in Larger Competitions Leads to More Cheating," *Organizational Behavior and Human Decision Processes* 164 (2021): 102–115.

28. S. Wiley Wakeman, Celia Moore, and Francesca Gino, "A Counterfeit Competence: After Threat, Cheating Boosts One's Self-Image," *Journal of Experimental Social Psychology* 82 (May 2019): 253–265.

29. Wakeman, Moore, and Gino, "A Counterfeit Competence."

30. Julia Lee, Ashley Hardin, Bidhan Parmar, and Francesca Gino, "How Dishonesty Drains You," *Scientific American* (October 2, 2019).

31. https://www.newyorker.com/magazine/2023/10/09/they-studied-dishonesty-was-their-work-a-lie.

32. C. Moore and F. Gino, "Approach, Ability, Aftermath: A Psychological Process Framework of Unethical Behavior at Work," *Academy of Management Annals* 9 (2015): 235–289.

33. J. J. Lee and F. Gino, "In Search of Moral Equilibrium: Person, Situation, and Their Interplay in Behavioral Ethics," in *The Atlas of Moral Psychology: Mapping Good and Evil in the Mind*, ed. K. Gray and J. Graham (Guilford Press, 2017).

34. Maryam Kouchaki and Francesca Gino, "Memories of Unethical Actions Become Obfuscated over Time," *Proceedings of the National Academy of Sciences* 113, no. 22 (May 31, 2016).

35. Francesca Gino and Maryam Kouchaki, "We're Unethical at Work Because We Forget Our Misdeeds," *Harvard Business Review* (May 18, 2016).

36. https://fee.org/articles/the-behavioral-experiment-that-helps-explain-the-fall-of-elizabeth-holmes-and-the-horrors-of-socialism.

37. Nicole E. Ruedy, Celia Moore, Francesca Gino, and Maurice Schweitzer, "The Cheater's High: The Unexpected Affective Benefits of Unethical Behavior," *Journal of Personality and Social Psychology* 105, no. 4 (October 2013): 531–548.

38. F. Gino, S. Ayal, and D. Ariely, "Self-serving Altruism? The Lure of Unethical Actions That Benefit Others," *Journal of Economic Behavior & Organization* 93 (September 2013): 285–292.

39. https://www.newyorker.com/magazine/2023/10/09/they-studied-dishonesty-was-their-work-a-lie.

40. https://www.newyorker.com/magazine/2023/10/09/they-studied-dishonesty-was-their-work-a-lie.

41. Ariely, *The (Honest) Truth About Dishonesty*, 47.

42. Ariely, *The (Honest) Truth About Dishonesty*, 49.

43. https://www.science.org/content/article/fraudulent-data-set-raise-questions-about-superstar-honesty-researcher.

# Notes

44. https://www.npr.org/2023/07/27/1190568472/dan-ariely-francesca-gino-harvard-dishonesty-fabricated-data.

45. F. Gino, M. Norton, and D. Ariely, "The Counterfeit Self: The Deceptive Costs of Faking It," *Psychological Science* 21, no. 5 (2010): 712–720.

46. Ariely, *The (Honest) Truth About Dishonesty*, 123.

47. F. Gino, *Sidetracked: Why Our Decisions Get Derailed and How We Can Stick to the Plan* (Harvard Business Review Press, 2013).

48. M. H. Bazerman and D. Chugh, "Decisions Without Blinders," *Harvard Business Review*, January 2006,

49. M. R. Banaji, M. H. Bazerman, and D. Chugh, "How (Un)ethical Are You?," *Harvard Business Review*, December 2003.

50. Eugenie S. Reich, *Plastic Fantastic: How the Biggest Fraud in Physics Shook the Scientific World* (Palgrave Macmillan, 2009).

51. https://www.ebsco.com/research-starters/physics/inquiry-reveals-physicist-jan-hendrik-schon-faked-his-research.

52. https://datacolada.org/109.

53. See D. Moore, P. Tetlock, L. Tanlu, and M. H. Bazerman, "Conflicts of Interest and the Case of Auditor Independence: Moral Seduction and Strategic Issue Cycling," *Academy of Management Review* 31, no. 1 (2006): 1–20, for an overview.

## Chapter 12

1. Nick Chater and George Loewenstein, "The I-Frame and the S-Frame: How Focusing on Individual-Level Solutions Has Led Behavioral Public Policy Astray," *Behavioral and Brain Sciences* 46 (2023): e147.

2. Leif D. Nelson, Joseph P. Simmons, and Uri Simonsohn, "Psychology's Renaissance," *Annual Review of Psychology* 69 (2018): 511–534.

3. Nelson, Simmons, and Simonsohn, "Psychology's Renaissance."

4. Nelson, Simmons, and Simonsohn, "Psychology's Renaissance."

5. Nelson, Simmons, and Simonsohn, "Psychology's Renaissance."

6. https://osf.io/hadz3.

7. Nelson, Simmons, and Simonsohn, "Psychology's Renaissance."

8. Max H. Bazerman, *Complicit: How We Enable the Unethical and How to Stop* (Princeton University Press, 2022).

9. Bazerman, *Complicit*.

10. And in the journals *Clinical Psychological Science* and *Advances in Methods and Practices in Psychological Science*.

11. https://journals.sagepub.com/doi/10.1177/09567976231221573.

12. Nelson, Simmons, and Simonsohn, "Psychology's Renaissance."

13. https://journals.sagepub.com/doi/10.1177/09567976231221573.

14. https://journals.sagepub.com/doi/10.1177/09567976231221573.

15. https://journals.sagepub.com/doi/10.1177/09567976231221573.

16. https://journals.sagepub.com/doi/10.1177/09567976231221573.

17. https://www.sciencedirect.com/science/article/abs/pii/S0749597824000037.

18. M. K. Noordewier, "Support for Those Affected by Scientific Misconduct Is Crucial." *Nature Human Behavior* 7 (2023): 830.

19. Noordewier, "Support for Those Affected by Scientific Misconduct Is Crucial."

20. https://www.faspe-ethics.org.

21. International Programs—Historical Estimates of World Population—U.S. Census Bureau, 2013-03-06.

# Index

Ability, 15
Acland, Erinn, 86–87
Advice taking, 17–18
Allen, Luke, 120
Amir, On, 24
Anaya, Jordan, 94
Andre, Quentin, 121
Ariely, Dan, 23, 131, 136
   and Bazerman, 23–24, 116
   and Gino, 23
   and Mazer, 25–26
   research, 23–24, 47, 115, 129, 137–142
   signing-first paper, 1–13, 25–26, 50–54, 56–59, 61–66, 75–78, 81, 82, 84, 86, 99
AsCollected, 150
AsPredicted.org, 147
Attia, Tim, 48
Ayal, Shahar, 140

Badges, 151
Baer, Mike, 153
Balachandra, Lakshmi, 84
Banaji, Mahzarin, 120, 143
Bargh, John, 36–37
Baserman, Stu, 11, 12, 47–48, 123
Bazerman, Max (author)
   and Ariely, 23–24
   and Balachandra, 84
   career, 2–3, 39–40

complicity, 26–27, 54, 142–143, 148–150
and Data Colada, 1–2, 57–61, 64–66, 113, 116–117, 119
and FASPE, 156–157
and Gino, 16–21, 61–62, 72–72, 81–82, 85
and Harvard investigation, 62–63, 66–67, 69–70, 116
interviews with Gino and Stapel co-authors, 101–102, 108, 117
Many Co-authors Project, 114, 122–123
and Mazar, 25–26
and Moore, 112–113
online-honesty project, 48–49
signing-first paper, 5–6, 8–10, 45–46, 49–54, 125
Slice Labs, 47–48, 123
and Stapel, 89
and Shu, 21–22
and Zeelenberg, 89, 103
Becker, Gary, 131
Behavioral economics, 30, 127, 145
Behavioral ethics, ix, 5, 17, 19, 143
Behavioral Insights Group, 20, 46
Behavioural Insights Team (BIT), 46–47, 125
Bell Labs, 143
Bem, Daryl, 30–33
Benevolence, 15–16

Bentham, Jeremy, 131
"Best 40 under 40" B-school list, 21, 25
*Better, Not Perfect: A Realist's Guide to Maximum Sustainable Goodness*, 5
BEworks, Inc., 7, 25
Bhanot, Syon, 125
Bhattacharjee, Yudhijit, 135
*Blind Spots: Why We Fail to Do What's Right and What to Do About It*, 5
Bohnet, Iris, 20
Borsboom, Denny, 98, 135
Bounded awareness, 143
Bounded ethicality, 19, 143
Brooks, Alison Wood, 109
Brown, Nick, 94
Burd, Greg, 19–20, 142
Bush administration, 5

Cacioppo, John, 135
Carney, Dana, 38
Casciaro, Tiziana, 55
Center for Open Science (COS), 40, 147
Chater, Nick, 145
Cheater's high, 140
Cheating on tests, 24
Chen, Frances, 109–110
Child abuse, 27
Chugh, Dolly, 4, 143
Chui, Celia, 138
Cialdini, Robert, 89
Co-authors, 101–117
  anonymous, 117
  and Gino, 3, 19, 61, 74, 108–117, 126, 141
  Many Co-authors Project, 72, 114, 122–123
  responsibilities of, 142–143, 148–151
  and Sanna, 92
  signing-first paper, ix–x, 1–2, 8–11, 13, 18–19, 26, 50, 54, 57–58, 65–66, 99, 125
  and Stapel, 102–108, 155
  trust in, 3, 8, 10, 15, 20, 25–7, 47, 53, 72, 113, 126, 135, 149, 151
  university support for, 155
*Collabra: Psychology*, 43
Colleagues, 15, 126, 140, 143, 149, 151, 154, 155. *See also* Co-authors
Collins, Hanne, 109
Competition, 135, 138–139
*Complicit: How We Enable the Unethical and How to Stop*, x, 3, 5, 13, 25–27, 143, 148, 156
Complicity, 14, 25–27, 54, 142–143, 148–150, 157
Cornell University, 94–95
Counterfeit goods, 141–142
COVID-19 pandemic, 21, 54
Creativity, 137–138
Credibility crisis in psychology, 29, 30, 37, 38
Criminal behavior, 131
Cross-cultural experience, 138
Cuddy, Amy, 38–39, 41–42

"Dark Side of Creativity: Original Thinkers Can Be More Dishonest, The," 138
Data Colada, x, 1–2, 11, 12–13, 32, 38–40, 57, 111
  AsCollected, 150
  attitudes toward, 42–43
  "Clusterfake," 70
  "Evidence of Fraud in an Influential Field Experiment About Dishonesty," 1, 60, 62–66, 71, 76
  Gino lawsuit, 41–42, 79–81, 85, 87, 107, 111–112
  and Gino papers, 61, 70–72
  Gino's critique of, 82, 83
  GoFundMe project, 119–122
  p-hacking paper of 2011, 33–35, 106, 132
  "Psychology's Renaissance," 41, 146
  replication review paper of 2018, 41

Index

Study 1 fraud allegation, 3, 70–71
Study 3 fraud allegation, 3, 24, 59, 60
Data fabrication allegations, 2, 18, 89–100. *See also* Co-authors; P-hacking
and collusion, 148–149
and data review, 150
Duke University, 77
Gino co-authored papers, 71–72, 74–75
Gonzalez, Roxana, 90
The Hartford's statement, 75–77
Hauser, Marc, 90, 93–94, 99
malicious actor, 85–86
motivation for, 136–137
Qualtrics files, 79–80
repercussions of, 125–126, 132–133
Ruggierio, Karen, 90, 99
Sanna, Lawrence, 90–92, 99
Smeesters, Dirk, 90–91, 99
Stapel, Diederik, 89–90, 95–99, 132–135
transparency, 100
Wansink, Brian, 90, 94–95, 99
Datar, Srikant, 70, 79, 85
Davis, Jim, 15
Dawson, Erica, 121
DeBellis, Mark, 120
Delta Dental, 23
*Derailed (Ontsporing)*, 98, 133
Diffusion of responsibility, 27
Disclosure, 146–148, 151–152
"Dishonest Deed, Clear Conscience: When Cheating Leads to Moral Disengagement and Motivated Forgetting," 18
Dishonesty, 136–141. *See also* Data fabrication allegations
"Dishonesty Explained: What Leads Moral People to Act Immorally," 86
Doner, Vicki, 121
Dorison, Charlie, 109
Doyen, Stéphane, 36–37

Drolet Rossi, Aimee, 24
Duke University, 1, 7, 23, 75, 77–78
Dweck, Carol, 30

Eich, Eric, 151
Eijlander, Philip, 96
Electric shocks experiment, 23
eMBeD, 25
Embodied cognition, 91
Endowment effect, 22
Equity, 148
Erasmus University, 90–91
Ethics. *See also* Rules; Unethical behavior
behavioral, 5, 17, 45
breakdown in society, 156
bounded ethicality, 19, 143
study of, 136
utilitarian, 132
Evers, Ellen, 95–96, 105–107
"Evidence of Fraud in an Influential Field Experiment About Dishonesty," 1, 60, 64–66, 71
*Evilicious: Why We Evolved a Taste for Being Bad*, 94
Experimental psychology, 32
Extrasensory perception (ESP), 32

Fabrication, 39. *See also* Data fabrication
Falsification, 39
Fellowships at Auschwitz for the Study of Professional Ethics (FASPE), 156
Flake, Jessica, 107, 119
Food choice research, 94
Fountain, Nick, 75
Francesca-v-harvard.org, 82–83, 111
Fraud. *See* Data fabrication
Frei, Francis, 80
Freud, Sigmund, 29

Galak, Jeff, 32
Germany, 157
Gilbert, Dan, 21–22, 40–41, 135

Gilovich, Tom, 106
Gino, Francesca, 1–13, 16–21, 23, 55–57, 126, 136–137
  and Ariely, 6,
  and Bazerman, 61–62, 81–82, 85, 150
  co-authors, 101–102, 108–117
  Data Colada accusations, 2–3, 70–72, 82–85
  Harvard investigation, 69–70, 86, 154–155
  lawsuit, 13, 41–42, 79–82, 85–87, 99, 107, 111–112, 119–122
  research, 72–75, 99, 122–124, 137–142
  signing-first paper, 6–10, 25, 50–54, 58, 61–67
Gino-Data Colada lawsuit, 13, 41–42, 79–82, 85, 87, 99, 107, 111–112, 119–122
Gino-Harvard Business School lawsuit, 42, 79, 82, 85–87
GoFundMe project, 119–122
Goldenberg, Amit, 48
Goldman, David, 156
Gonzalez, Roxana, 90
Grant, Adam, 19, 30

Habitual behavior, 139
Halpern, Daniel, 46, 125
Hamakor, 24
Hardin, Ashley, 139
Hardwicke, Tom E., 152–153
The Hartford Insurance Company, 75, 141
Harvard Business School (HBS), ix, 80, 90
  *Crimson* op-ed, 85
  Gino and, 2, 12, 16, 17–21
  Gino investigation, 2–3, 61–63, 66–67, 69–74, 82, 84, 115–117, 126, 154–155
  Gino lawsuit, 42, 79, 82, 85–87
  lab management, 150

Negotiation, Organizations and Markets (NOM) unit, 16, 21, 54, 62, 82, 125–126
  Slice Labs case, 48–49
Harvard University
  Behavioral Insights Group, 20, 46
  Hauser investigation, 93
  and MIT, 23
Hauser, Marc, 12, 39, 90, 93–94, 99, 136, 154–155
*Hidden Potential: The Science of Achieving Great Things*, 30
Hildreth, Angus, 72
Holmes, Elizabeth, 140, 148
*(Honest) Truth About Dishonesty, The*, 23, 142
"Hot Potato," 35
Huang, Karen, 109

Implicit complicity, 148–149
Inbar, Yoel, 81, 95–96, 105–107, 119
In-principle acceptance, 152
Institute for Replication (I4R), 152–153
Insurance industry
  The Hartford's statement, 75–77
  mileage reporting, 7–8, 50, 59, 149
  online claimants, 48
  signing-first study, 5–10, 26, 50–51, 56–59, 61, 75–78, 82
Integrity, 15–16
Internal Revenue Service (IRS), 148

James, William, 29, 32
Jeong, Martha, 109
Jobs, Steve, 137
John, Leslie, 36
Johnson, Otto, 120
Joun, Myong J., 87
*Journal of Experimental Psychology: Learning, Memory, and Cognition*, 40
*Journal of Personality and Social Psychology*, 30, 40
Journal rules, 151–153

# Index

Kahneman, David, 30, 37–38, 41, 83
Kalnins, Arturs, 121
King, Gary, 40
Kohlberg, Lawrence, 131
Kouchaki, Maryam, 55, 138, 140, 153
Kristal, Ariella, 11, 48–51, 54, 65–66

Lageman, Thessa, 91
Laibson, David, 89
Lawsuit. See Gino-Data Colada lawsuit; Gino-Harvard Business School lawsuit
LeBel, Etienne, 32
LeBoeuf, Robyn A., 32
Lee, Julia, 139
Lemonade, 47
Lessig, Lawrence, 80
Levelt, William, 103
Levelt Committee, 103–107
Lewis-Kraus, Gideon, 81–82, 84, 141
Liljenquist, Katie, 56
Lindsey, Stephen, 152
Lodge, Jennifer, 77
Loewenstein, George, 24, 36, 145
Luca, Michael, 46

Macbeth effect, 55–56
Madoff, Bernie, 139
Many Co-authors Project, 72, 114, 122–124
Maximizing utility, 132
Mazar, Nina, 1, 6–11, 24–26, 50–54, 57–58, 64–65, 85–86, 149
McCallum, Robert, 5
Mensch, Jeffrey I., 121
Mesmerism, 29
Meyer, Roger, 15
Milkman, Katy, 4
Miltenberg, Andrew, 87
*Mindset: The New Psychology of Success*, 30
Minson, Julia, 109–112, 114, 122
MIT, 23, 25, 36

Monkey behavior, 92–93
Moore, Celia, 139
Moore, Don, 4, 17–19, 111–114, 119–122
*Moral Minds: The Nature of Right and Wrong*, 94
Moral psychologists, 136
Moran, Joseph D., 121

Nazi Germany, 157
Neale, Maggie, 115
Negotiation, Organizations and Markets (NOM) unit, 16, 21, 54, 82, 125–126
Nelson, Leif D., 1–2, 32–33, 43, 64, 79, 99, 105–106, 113, 146
Networking, 55
Noordewier, Marret, 107–108, 155–156
Norton, Mike, 142
Nosek, Brian, 40–41, 43, 80–81, 119, 156
*Nudge*, 45–46
Nudges, 5, 45–46
Nudge Unit, 125

Online honesty study, 48–50
*Ontsporing (Derailed)*, 98, 133
Open science movement, 17, 40, 43, 127, 149, 153–154
*Organizational Behavior and Human Decision Processes*, 21, 73, 153
Osf.io, 147
Outliers, data, 34–35

Parmar, Bidhan, 139
*Perspectives on Psychological Science*, 42
Peters, Kurt, 32
Pettigrew, Stephen, 40
P-hacking, 33–40, 43, 56, 84, 94, 113, 133, 146, 151
    Data Colada paper of 2011, 33–35, 106, 132
Phrenology, 29

Physiognomy, 29
Picasso, Pablo, 137
Plagiarism, 84–87
"Policy Challenges of Behavioral Science Research," 89
*Power of Experiments, The,* 46
Power posing, 38–39
Precognition, 32–33
*Predictably Irrational,* 23
Prelec, Drazen, 36
Preregistration, 33, 146–147, 150, 153
*Presence: Bringing Your Boldest Self to Your Biggest Challenges,* 38
Priming studies, 36–38
Promotion/prevention mindset, 55
Psychoanalysis, 29
*Psychological Science,* 40, 43, 71, 72, 127, 146, 151–154
Psychology, 29–30
  development of, 30, 146, 151
  disclosure and replication, 152–153
  replicability crisis, 39–44
  research credibility, 29–30, 37–38, 145–146
"Psychology's Renaissance," 41, 146, 151
Psychotherapy, 29

Randomization failure, 50, 53, 57, 59, 62, 65
Ranehill, Eva, 38
Rationality, 127
*Rebel Talent,* 86, 137, 138
Registered reports, 152
Relationships, 15–16, 26–27, 53, 126, 143
Replicability crisis, 39–44
Replication-failure paper of 2020, 11, 25, 50–51, 54, 61
Research Transparency Statement, 153
RICO tobacco trial, 5
Rogers, Todd, 4

Romariz, Alexandre S., 120
Ross, Lee, 109
Ruggiero, Karen, 90, 99
Rules, 129–133
  breaking, 131–133, 137–138
  and creativity, 138
  journal, 151–153
  purpose of, 130–131
Ryan, William, 121

Sackler family, 148
Salsbury, Daniel, 52, 54
Sanders, Michael, 3–4, 46–47, 125
Sanna, Lawrence, 39, 90–92, 99
Saribay, Adil, 121
Scheiber, Noam, 83–84
Schindler, Oskar, 132
Schön, Jan Hendrik, 143
Schoorman, David, 15
Schroeder, Juliana, 122
Schwartz, Barry, 89
Schwarz, Norbert, 38, 41
Schweitzer, Maurice, 74, 122
Schwitzgebel, Eric, 136
Scientific method, 29, 32, 33, 94, 121, 130, 132
Self-correcting nature of science, 42
Sexism, 41–42
Sezer, Ovul, 21, 72, 73
Shafir, Eldar, 89
Shakespeare, William, 137
Shu, Lisa, 1, 6, 8–13, 18, 21–22, 25, 46, 50, 54, 57–59, 61, 62, 64–66, 73, 141, 150
*Sidetracked,* 86, 142
"Signing at the Beginning Makes Ethics Salient and Decreases Dishonest Self-Reports in Comparison to Signing at the End" (signing-first paper of 2012), 1, 19
  BIT studies, 46–47
  citations, 45
  effects of, 3–4

insurance company study (Study 3), 1, 3, 5–13, 24–26, 50–51, 53, 56–59, 61, 75–78, 82, 86, 141
lab studies (Study 1, Study 2), 2–3, 6–7, 13, 49, 50–51, 56, 61, 63, 65–67, 70, 83, 150
and online honesty study, 49–50
online implementation, 47–49
repercussions of, 123–127
replication-failure paper of 2020, 11, 25, 50–51, 54, 61
retraction of, x, 3, 13, 52–54, 57–58, 61–62, 64–66, 69, 74, 79, 86, 116, 119
timeline, 12–13, 141
Silence, 156–157
Simmons, Joseph P., 1–2, 32–35, 38, 62, 64, 66, 79, 99, 105–106, 119, 146
Simonsohn, Uri, 1–2, 10, 33–35, 38–39, 42, 62, 64, 66, 74, 79, 90–92, 99, 105–106, 109, 119, 122, 146, 148, 150
Slice Labs, 47–48, 123
Smeesters, Dirk, 39, 90–91, 99
Smith, Michael, 93
*Social and Behavioral Sciences Team Annual Report*, 45
Social psychology, 30, 36, 41, 91, 109. *See also* Psychology
Social science, 29, 125
and Bem paper, 32–33
credibility of, x, 3, 11, 14, 16, 29, 157
and data fabrication, 126
diffusion of responsibility in, 27
field experiments, 46
and p-hacking, 34, 39–40
and rationality, 127
and replication failures, 40–44
reform movement in, 11, 39, 41, 45, 113–114, 148, 153–154
self-correction, 42
statistical significance, 33–34
and universities, 154

Society for the Improvement of Psychological Science (SIPS), 43, 127
Spellman, Barbara, 42
Spiritualism, 29
Stapel, Diederik, 39, 89, 95–99, 102–108, 129, 133–135, 137, 139, 155
Statistical significance, 33–35
Statistics, transparency, and rigor (STAR), 152
Steroid use, 132
Sunstein, Cass, 45

Tax compliance paper of 2017, 47
Tenbrunsel, Ann, 5, 19
Ten Commandments study, 24
Thaler, Richard, 24, 45, 120
*Thinking, Fast and Slow*, 30
Tilburg Institute conference, 89
Tilburg University, 97, 103–105, 135, 155
Timeline of scandal, 12–13
Transparency, 43, 65, 77–78, 93, 100, 150–153
Trust
bases of, 15–16
in co-authors, 3, 8, 10, 20, 25–7, 47, 53, 72, 113, 126, 135, 149, 151
and complicity, 148
and relationships, 15, 26
in social science, 3–4, 66, 135
and verification, 27
Tuckfield, Bradford, 101, 136

Unethical behavior, 5, 14, 85
and cheater's high, 140
clinical basis of, 139–140
and competition, 138–139
and creativity, 137–138
and ego, 139
and habit, 139
and helping others, 140–141
and overcommitment, 139

Unethical behavior (cont.)
　and p-hacking, 39
　slippery slope of, 17
　and trust, 27
Universities, x, 30, 40, 43, 74, 98, 105, 108, 122, 129, 132, 146, 153–156
University of Amsterdam, 97, 155
University of Groningen, 97, 155
University of Michigan, 92
University of North Carolina, 6, 92
U.S. Department of Health and Human Services, 93
Utilitarianism, x, 132

van der Zee, Tim, 94
van Wolferen, Job, 95–96, 105–107
Vazire, Simine, 42–43, 107, 119–120, 127, 152–153
Vincent, Lynne, 138

Wagenmakers, Eric-Jan, 98, 135
Wakeman, Wiley, 139
Wansink, Brian, 90, 94–95, 99
Weatherby, Leif, 126–127
Weight-on-advice (WOA), 17–18
Weinstein, Harvey, 148
"When I'm 64," 35
Whillans, Ashley, 11, 12, 13, 48–49, 50, 51, 54, 59, 62, 65–66
Whistleblowers, 157
Wilson, Matt, 22
Wilson, Tim, 40
Wiltermuth, Scott, 114–116, 138

Yap, Andy, 38
Yeomans, Mike, 109

Zeelenberg, Marcel, 89, 96, 102–105, 107
Zhang, Ting, 21, 72
Zhong, Chen-Bo, 56
Ziani, Zoé, 55–57